THE NEW EASTERN EUROPE

THE NEW EASTERN EUROPE
WESTERN RESPONSES

J.M.C. Rollo
with
Judy Batt
Brigitte Granville
Neil Malcolm

PUBLISHED IN NORTH AMERICA FOR

THE ROYAL INSTITUTE OF INTERNATIONAL AFFAIRS

COUNCIL ON FOREIGN RELATIONS PRESS
• NEW YORK •

Chatham House Papers

General Series Editor: William Wallace

The Royal Institute of International Affairs, at Chatham House in London, has provided an impartial forum for discussion and debate on current international issues for 70 years. Its resident research fellows, specialized information resources, and range of publications, conferences, and meetings span the fields of international politics, economics, and security. The Institute is independent of government.

Chatham House Papers are short monographs on current policy problems which have been commissioned by the RIIA. In preparing the papers, authors are advised by a study group of experts convened by the RIIA, and publication of a paper indicates that the Institute regards it as an authoritative contribution to the public debate. The Institute does not, however, hold opinions of its own; the views expressed in this publication are the responsibility of the author.

Library of Congress Cataloguing-in-Publication Data

Rollo, J.M.C.
    The new Eastern Europe: western responses/by J.M.C. Rollo, with Judy Batt, Brigitte Granville, and Neil Malcolm.
        p.   cm.
    "Published in North America for the Royal Institute of International Affairs."
    ISBN 0-87609-085-4 : $14.95
    1. Europe, Eastern—Politics and government—1989– 2. Europe, Eastern—Economic conditions—1989– I. Royal Institute of International Affairs. II. Title.
DJK51.5.R65 1990
947—dc20
                                                    90—34197
                                                    CIP

90 91 92 93 94 95 96 PB 10 9 8 7 6 5 4 3 2 1

CONTENTS

ACKNOWLEDGMENTS

I should like to thank all of those who have contributed to the preparation of this paper. It benefited from discussion in a series of study groups set up by the Royal Institute of International Affairs at Chatham House, and my thanks go to all from inside and outside Chatham House who found time to attend and contribute. The study group was much helped by specially prepared papers from David Dyker (University of Sussex) on the USSR, George Blazyca (Thames Polytechnic) on Poland, Paul Hare (Heriot-Watt University) on Hungary, Ian Jeffries (University of Swansea) on the German Democratic Republic and Ludek Rychetnik (University of Reading) on Czechoslovakia.

I thank my joint authors, Judy Batt, Brigitte Granville, Neil Malcolm and Hope Roper, for forbearance in the face of unreasonable deadlines; John Roper for continuous encouragement; Pauline Wickham for editorial guidance; and Lisa Allyn, Shyama Iyer and Marie Lathia for secretarial assistance. Midland Montagu and the Tokyo Club Foundation for Global Studies provided financial support. All faults remain the responsibility of the authors.

March 1990   J.M.C. Rollo

1
INTRODUCTION

J.M.C. Rollo

As the societies of Eastern Europe emerge from the wreckage of forty years of Leninism, they need help in building democratic structures and market economies. Their needs are pressing, but the task is enormous and the timescale for change is long. What can the West do? What should the West do? What is the West doing and how do its actions measure up? This survey attempts to answer these questions by examining why change has occurred in Eastern Europe at this juncture, why the previous system failed, what the East Europeans are proposing to put in its place, what policy instruments in the hands of the West may help, and what has been done and what more needs to be done. But before we turn to a chapter-by-chapter summary, we need to define the terms 'Eastern Europe' and 'the West', as well as to offer a word of explanation on the Soviet Union.

The geographical labelling of the countries east of the Elbe is a matter of great sensitivity. In the days of the Soviet bloc it was easy and not inaccurate to describe anywhere in Europe that was east of the West German, Austrian and Italian borders as Eastern Europe. That has now changed. The four countries used here as case-studies – Poland, Hungary, Czechoslovakia and the German Democratic Republic – consider themselves to be Central or East-Central Europeans. The area in the process of change, however, includes the Balkan states, and so perhaps – in that all embracing sense – the term Eastern Europe is still a useful shorthand. It is used as such in this volume. It indicates that although the detailed analysis is based on systems and events in four countries only, the general conclusions will have wider relevance when, as is inevitable, the West becomes deeply involved in the process of change in the Balkans.

As for 'the West', this grouping is less difficult to define, although the term is not necessarily more logical. It embraces the 24 countries of the OECD plus the multilateral organizations of which they – but also others – are members, notably the IMF, the World Bank, the GATT, the European Community and the OECD itself. The full range is set out in Table 6.1.

Finally, the Soviet Union has been given a separate chapter, partly because, as a regional superpower, it is a potential instigator of change in Eastern Europe, and partly because, as a society itself in process of change, it too is a potential beneficiary of Western support.

Chapter 2 examines the political context of change in previously socialist societies. This is the crucial analytical chapter of the book because it describes how Leninist political structures undermined all previous attempts at economic reform in Eastern Europe, and hence why political change is necessary for economic reform to take place. This chapter gives strong support to the view that there is no effective middle path, or 'third way', between communism and welfare capitalism as it has developed in Western Europe in the postwar period. The chapter also discusses the events that led to the changes in the four countries chosen for study and suggests some future scenarios.

Chapters 3 and 4 deal directly with the economic dimension. They build on the view that economic change can take place only if the old Leninist structures are removed. Chapter 3 sets out the economic framework which is needed to underpin reform, and stresses the importance of an open pricing system. Other essential features are the right to property ownership, an effective system of civil and commercial law, an effective competition policy, including open frontiers, a well-defined public sector subject to democratic control, and a stable currency. It further examines the recent economic history of Poland, Hungary, Czechoslovakia and the GDR.

Chapter 4 turns to the process of reform and looks at progress to date in each country. It argues that where there are problems at the macroeconomic level, notably with the balance of payments externally and inflation internally, these should be tackled immediately but as part of the framework of wider economic reform. Thus increased exchange-rate convertibility and a more open trade policy will both assist stabilization and promote structural change. Similarly, the development of capital markets will allow domestic monetary policy to be effective as well as providing a means of mobilizing savings and funding profitable investment. The chapter argues that the priorities for structural reform are opening up the goods markets to competition from overseas, and reforming domestic legal structures to allow private property and bankruptcy as well as introducing laws on overseas investment, accountancy standards and capital markets. The discussion of the GDR concentrates on monetary unification with the FRG and its implications for the reform process.

The role of the Soviet Union is discussed in Chapter 5. The chapter addresses two questions. First, how different is the USSR from the smaller countries of Eastern Europe, and can it be treated in the same way? Second, what is the likely role of the Soviet Union in the region, and how are the West's actions likely to influence its behaviour? The broad answer to the first question is that by reason of size alone the USSR is different, even though the economic and political problems it faces are the same as those faced by the East Europeans. The second question requires a more conditional answer: it depends on the nature of the Soviet leadership. A more nationalistic, less accommodating regime than that led by Mr Gorbachev could put at risk large-scale disarmament. More generally, it could intervene disruptively in Eastern Europe. Because of its size and its lagging position on economic and political reform, the USSR is not yet eligible for the kind of close relationship on offer to some East Europeans. It must not, however, be excluded from Western concerns. Progress on the CFE and CSCE processes, close contacts with Western economic and political organizations – notably the IMF, the World Bank, the GATT, the Council of Europe and the European Community – would all help to prevent the USSR from being isolated.

The West's policy options, and options for action, are discussed in Chapters 6, 7 and 8. Chapter 6 examines the range of policies available to the West and the constraints on their use. At one level, the use of the term 'policies' is misleading in that it suggests government action. In this case, the main task is to activate the private sector in Eastern Europe. The key to that task is domestic and foreign private investment. Western governments can do relatively little directly to control the behaviour of the Western private sector, which will depend crucially on the internal incentives in Eastern Europe and access to world markets. The two areas where greater certainty would be welcome are those where Western action is most constrained. The first is debt relief, where the West is constrained from forgiving East European debt not just by the scale of the problem but by possible demonstration effects in the rest of the world. The second issue is the integration of East European economies into the world economy, the role of Europe in general and the EC in particular. The chapter argues that close integration into a wider European economy, and in particular access to the four freedoms of movement – of goods (including agriculture), services, capital and labour – would give the best long-term guarantee that selective trade policy would not be used against the East Europeans just at the point at which they were becoming competitive in world markets. This raises the issue of full EC membership, which, on the economic front at least, may hold fewer fears for the East Europeans than it does for others, since they need to move to a new system of regulation anyway. The political constraints on the Community side, however, put severe limits on how far eventual membership can be contemplated.

Chapter 7 considers Western policy to date in each country. It concludes that policy is reasonably well directed to the immediate problems confronting Hungary and Poland, where the issues have been under consideration for some time. For Czechoslovakia and the GDR the issues are different. In the former, no serious macro-economic problem has as yet been detected, and the priority is to bring it within the world economic system and to encourage the private sector to invest. For the GDR, reunification with the Federal Republic will allow a much swifter integration into the European economy than is possible for any other East European country. This will be accelerated by a rapid move to a currency union.

Chapter 7 also identifies a potentially serious coordination problem with 24 governments, up to seven multilateral agencies and countless non-governmental agencies potentially active in Eastern Europe. It concludes that the European Commission, if not initially the most obvious institution to take the coordinator role, should continue to act in this capacity. As the number of East European countries eligible for help increases, the need for strong analytical and operational skills inside the Commission will increase, as will the need for clear lines of responsibility.

The final chapter looks ahead to some of the likely emerging problems in Eastern Europe and at possible Western responses.

2

THE POLITICAL CONTEXT*

Judy Batt

The political obstacles to economic reform
The introduction of market-type economic reforms into communist states cannot succeed without simultaneous political reform; that is the lesson from the experience of the past three decades of unsuccessful attempts at reform. In the classic 'Leninist' model, which characterized the East European states up to 1989, politics was inseparable from economics in the most direct and literal sense. The economy was overwhelmingly state-owned and state-directed through the command planning system, while the state itself was completely subordinate to the Communist Party. The Party effectively took over the market's vital stimulatory, organizational and disciplinary functions in all areas of the economy. The communist form of dictatorship was thus fundamentally different from traditional autocracies and authoritarian regimes, which have always coexisted with a market economy and a substantial degree of private ownership, even where state intervention in the economy has been extensive. Dismantling the dictatorships in Eastern Europe presents, therefore, a far more complex and far-reaching problem than that encountered in the cases of Spain and Portugal in the 1970s. This

* The sections on Poland and the GDR in this chapter have been contributed by Hope and John Roper.

6

will become clearer if we begin by considering the mechanisms by which the Party exercised its 'leading role' in the economic sphere in the classic Leninist system.

The Party did not manage the economy directly itself, but through the state apparatus – the government, the planning commission, and ministerial bureaucracies and enterprises, which, in an unreformed economy, were linked together hierarchically to form a complex but unified chain of command. The Party controlled recruitment, appointments and promotion throughout the state apparatus by means of the so-called *nomenklatura* system. This system related to one of the key tasks of the Party's secretarial apparatus (the full-time paid Party functionaries) at each level from the central through the various regional and district bodies: namely, to maintain lists of approved potential candidates for the various official posts (not only in the economy, but in education, the mass media, trade unions, etc.) which fell within their geographical area of responsibility.

Thus at the top level, the Secretariat of the Party's Central Committee, and ultimately the General Secretary himself, was responsible for nominating the Prime Minister and the government. These nominations were usually discussed and approved by the Party's top decision-making body, the Politburo or Presidium, before being presented to the Parliament for formal ratification. The Prime Minister and President (head of state) always also held seats on the Party's Politburo, and frequently the General Secretary combined his post as Party leader with that of President, or, less frequently after Khrushchev, with that of Prime Minister. There was thus substantial overlap at the top between the Party and the state leadership, but the Party leadership always retained the upper hand; the Prime Minister was at best second in rank in the Politburo, and may have been significantly less influential in policy-making than other individuals, particularly other Party Secretaries responsible for ideology, international and security matters, or economic affairs. The Prime Minister, and the government in general, should be seen as primarily concerned with the special responsibility for detailed, expert management of the economy according to basic policy priorities determined by the Party Politburo and approved by the Party's Central Committee. However, the government ministers worked closely on a day-to-day basis with the Party Central Committee's own parallel bureaucracy in its specialized Departments responsible for supervising the major branches of the

7

economy. These Departments appeared in fact to have the final say, their influence deriving from their direct linkage to the *nomenklatura* system.

At lower levels of the hierarchy, the regional and district Party apparatus was *de facto* responsible for the appointment and monitoring of people in managerial positions in every sphere of social and economic life within their area. This included enterprise managers, although formally enterprise managers were appointed by the branch ministry (a government ministry responsible for a particular industrial sector) to which the enterprise was subordinate. The appointment of senior management to particularly large and important enterprises was, however, usually controlled directly by the Central Committee apparatus. A major issue in appointments to managerial posts throughout the state economic bureaucracy was the relative weight to be attached to specialist expertise, formal qualifications and competence as against political loyalty and ideological 'soundness'. Although official publications on this subject always placed considerable emphasis on the need for competent and expert personnel in leading posts, the very fact that the point was regularly reiterated indicates that, in practice, political loyalty tended to outweigh all other criteria. Nevertheless, it should not be assumed that all occupants of managerial and executive positions were incompetent political hacks: because Party membership was virtually a precondition for a successful career in any field, bright and ambitious young people also aspired to membership of the Party, without necessarily accepting uncritically and *in toto* its ideology and political aims. However, Party membership entailed discipline and subordination to the goals set by the hierarchy, over which the rank-and-file member had little control; the penalties for stepping out of line were considerable where that same hierarchy also controlled one's career prospects. Obviously, this set of arrangements tended to foster attitudes of conformity and even servility.

The Party's 'leading role' in the day-to-day running of the economy was reinforced by the presence in every workplace, from central ministry to enterprise workshop, of Party groups or cells, organized by a local Party committee and a voluntary or full-time Party secretary (depending on the size of the membership and the importance of the location). At the level of the enterprise, therefore, the manager found himself working very closely with an enterprise Party secretary, whose role was both to aid the manager in the basic task of plan-fulfilment and to report on the manager's performance to the Party committee of the region within which his enterprise was situated. Managers were thus subject to dual subordination to both the branch ministry, from which they received plan directives and to which they reported on plan-fulfilment, and to the Party – either at the regional level or directly, at the level of the relevant department of the Central Committee apparatus.

The enterprise manager had a powerful incentive to maintain good relations with the enterprise Party secretary and regional Party apparatus because these had the power to make or break his career: for example, if (as frequently happened) the planned supplies of a particular input failed to materialize owing to some bottleneck beyond the control of either the manager or his branch ministry, the regional Party secretary would step in as a troubleshooter, and prevent a breakdown in production in one enterprise by raiding the stocks of another (in a lower-priority branch) within the given geographical region over which he had control. He thus fulfilled a vital interstitial function within the overcentralized and segmentalized economy, which was the source of his tremendous local influence. Through this process, very powerful local cliques, based on mutual interest, became established.[1] Naturally, this frequently led to corruption: enterprise managers diverted resources, for example, to build the local Party secretary a country cottage, and in return the manager was guaranteed priority access to scarce supplies and thus was able to report successful plan-fulfilment to his branch ministerial superiors, who in turn approved the manager's bonus or recommended him for promotion.

The Party's 'leading role' in the economy encompassed not only control over appointments and day-to-day supervision and intervention in management, but also of course, as suggested above, the making of policy itself. The role of Parliament was virtually non-existent, reduced to the largely ceremonial, passive function of formally approving, and thus lending a rather flimsy legitimacy to, major pieces of legislation. Parliamentary sessions were very brief and infrequent (typically only 2–4 days twice a year), and as a result there was no time for proper debate of major issues, even if the deputies had been so inclined – which, for the most part, they were not, being themselves creatures of the Party-controlled electoral process and thus subject to the same political constraints as other *nomenklatura* appointees.

The key policy-making body, after the Party Politburo, was the Central Committee, to which major issues were referred for debate (at closed sessions), and which, on the relatively rare occasions of an unresolved division or personal power struggle within the Politburo, could exercise a decisive role. The Central Committee's approval had to be sought for changes in the composition of the Politburo, and its support had to be sought for major policy changes. The Central Committee was formally elected by the quinquennial Party Congresses on the basis of nominations presented on behalf of the Politburo by the General Secretary, who thus had substantial, but by no means absolute, control over its political complexion. Its membership comprised a large proportion of *ex officio* representatives from all the major bureaucratic institutions: from the economic ministries and major enterprises to the armed services, trade unions and the Party's own central and regional apparatus. There would also be a few leading personalities from the cultural intelligentsia, possibly some of the General Secretary's personal favourites or even family members, and always the odd token 'worker' or 'peasant'.

This pattern of politics produces a remarkably close-knit, mutually self-supporting oligarchy at the centre, having well-established links with the interlocking cliques in the regions, all effectively screened from public scrutiny by near-total control over the mass media. Now, assuming the emergence at the top of the Party of a new leader or group committed to the introduction of economic reform, it is clear that such an oligarchy will be peculiarly ill-suited to the task of carrying it out, since the interests of a large number, if not most, of the individuals and groups within it are critically at stake. Many individuals stand to lose their positions of power, prestige and privilege; nearly all will have to adapt to new demands and a new, more exacting environment; most will be able to find convincing ideological grounds for opposing the introduction of alien 'capitalist' economic concepts into the socialist system.[2]

Past attempts at reform in Eastern Europe demonstrate that the introduction of economic reform requires more than merely extensive personnel changes throughout the apparatus: these are unlikely to guarantee a General Secretary intent on reform the sustained support he needs from the Central Committee in order to enforce his programme. In fact, a new type of leadership is needed with an altogether different power-base – the authority which derives from the support of a Parliament freely elected by the people in whose name the Party has claimed for so many years to rule. Electoral reform and the resuscitation of genuine parliamentary politics not only provide the essential underpinning for reformist leadership; they also serve as an invaluable source of information on the popular mood, and as a means of legitimating new policies and economic measures which may be far from universally welcomed among the wider public. An essential concomitant of this is the end of censorship, and the opening up of the press for the airing of a much greater variety of views. This will generate confidence in published information, and, it is to be hoped, contribute to winning hearts and minds for the cause of reform. As a result, the power of the vested bureaucratic interests opposing reform should be undercut.

Political reform must include the abandonment of the *nomenklatura* system and, by extension, the removal from their posts of political appointees who lack the requisite qualifications. The abolition of Party cells in the workplace is a further unavoidable measure if managerial responsibility is to be clearly defined, and if managers are to have the confidence needed to take risks and exercise initiative. Credible trade unions, free from Party manipulation, and elected workers' councils in enterprises must be established in order to generate confidence in the reform among the workforce. The removal of the oppressive atmosphere which has permeated workplace and society alike is, of course, an essential condition for releasing the creative energy and initiative from below which is vital to the success of economic reform. This also requires radical reform in the scope and functions of the internal security forces.

Finally, it will be clear that the logic of political reforms as outlined above tends inexorably towards the abandonment of the Party's 'leading role' itself, and its replacement by open, competitive politics and some form of multi-party system. Political stability and national consensus, key conditions for the successful and consistent implementation of economic reform, will therefore depend heavily on the formation of an effective alternative governing team from among the emergent new parties and movements, a team committed to, and in close agreement on, the principles of economic reform and enjoying the majority support of the population.

11

In the case studies below, we shall assess the current progress and future prospects of satisfactory political reform as defined above in each of the respective countries. This is treated in country studies below: in each of them we examine the extent to which the Communist Party has been dislodged from its leading role in the political system; we also present the basic outlines of the emerging party system, and discuss the prospects for the formation of effective and legitimate governments from the forthcoming elections, which will be, moreover, fully committed to economic reform.

POLAND

Recent developments in Poland have to be seen in the light of the earlier events of 1980–1, when the unofficial trade union, Solidarity, was briefly legalized and then suppressed under martial law.[3] Poland had had earlier popular disturbances – in 1956 and 1968. The events of 1988–9 might easily have been a rerun of 1980–1 but for the decisive factor of the totally changed Soviet attitude.

Developments in Poland must also be seen against a background of very severe economic problems, outdated industries and unproductive agriculture. In contrast with other East European countries, about three-quarters of Polish agricultural land is privately owned in some 2.7 million holdings, half of them farmed by peasants over or near retiring age. The overall population, however, is predominantly young, almost half being under thirty. The Roman Catholic Church is extremely strong, in urban as well as rural areas, and is closely linked to Solidarity.

Recent Polish history has left people very pessimistic about their future. An official poll taken just before the referendum, carried out by the communist government on its economic proposals in November 1987, showed 80% thinking the country's mood uneasy and also 80% with negative feelings towards the government. Some 60% thought there were reasons for a 'serious explosion' or open social conflict. The referendum had two questions: support for substantial economic reform (an attempt to get a mandate for the severe and painful changes needed), which attracted 64% of the poll; and support for the democratization of political life, which attracted 69%. The turnout, however, was only 67%, which meant that neither proposition was supported by the required 50% of the electorate.

1988 proceeded with the government mixing reform and repression. In March, for example, the police broke up a Peace and Freedom meeting (WiP), but at the same time the government approved alternatives to military service on other than medical grounds. Later it changed the military oath of allegiance to remove promises of loyalty to the Soviet Army.

Solidarity attempted to register legally as a trade union, but failed. The wage/price policy was opposed not only by Solidarity but also by OPZZ, the official trade union body, set up by the government after the imposition of martial law. Prices rose very steeply, leading to demands for wage rises, which were backed by strikes and demonstrations. An industrial price freeze at the end of March attempted to halt these wage increases. Strikes, however, escalated and General Jaruzelski realized, and admitted, that the country was at a turning-point. The Nowa Huta steel strike was broken by force, and Gdansk shipworkers, after a police siege, marched out after a nine-day sit-in to a service in St Brygida's Church with no agreement. Nevertheless, in the first five months of 1988 wages rose by 61%, 10% more than prices.

In August 1988 the big sit-ins in the mines took place, precipitating another crisis. The government was still opposed to the legalization of Solidarity, but was prepared to have round-table talks. Solidarity thought the table should be square rather than round – for negotiation on known problems, not just discussion. What they were seeking was pluralism, in trade union, social and political life, and the establishment of an agreement to deal with this immediate crisis. Despite talks about talks in September between Lech Walesa and other Solidarity leaders on the one side, and General Kiszczak, the Interior Minister, and Stanislaw Ciosek, a reforming member of the Politburo, on the other, the round table did not materialize. On 18 September the Messner government resigned, to be succeeded on 27 September by a new prime minister, Mieczyslaw Rakowski, who formed a government in mid-October. He had hoped to form a broad coalition but was not successful and had instead just the usual coalition of the Communists (Polish United Workers' Party) and the traditional partners from the smaller Peasants' Party (ZSL) and Democratic Party (SD), leaving three spaces vacant as a sign of his desire to attract wider support.

The troubled situation continued, exacerbated by the decision to close the Gdansk shipyard, over two years, as uneconomic. Since this was the cradle of Solidarity, it was seen by many as a deliberately provocative move, though Rakowski quoted a poll showing that 57.6% of Poles supported the closure of unprofitable enterprises including even the Gdansk shipyard. Meanwhile, although Solidarity was not legal, its profile became even higher. On 30 November Walesa appeared on Polish television for the first time since 1980–1, in a 45-minute live debate with Miodowicz, the OPZZ leader. At the end of December Solidarity formed its own shadow cabinet. Fifteen commissions were charged with all the main portfolios, including pluralism and the protection of the environment.

It was clear that the government and the Party had to talk to Solidarity, and in the end talks were arranged, not without difficulties, for 6 February 1989. In all, 57 people participated: from the Communist Party and its two allied parties, from Solidarity and OPZZ, and two Catholic priests. The talks took place against the background of continued industrial unrest. (In January there had been over 150 wage conflicts, 39 resulting in strikes or near-strikes.) Pietrzyk, a Solidarity miners' representative, even left the negotiations to resolve a strike in the lignite mines. Talks lasted until 5 April, when they were concluded with the legalization of Solidarity and the arrangement of a minority parliamentary role for the opposition.

The round-table agreement led to a rather complicated election in June 1989. The 100-seat Senate, in which Solidarity was free to contest all seats, was elected on the basis that to win in the first-round ballot required 50% plus one out of all the votes cast, with a run-off ballot, if needed, between the two highest candidates on a first-past-the-post basis. The agreement allocated the 460 seats in the Sejm, the lower and more powerful house, on the basis of 161 to non-establishment parties (in practice Solidarity) and the rest to the Communist Party (173 seats) and its two main allied parties (Peasants 78 and Democrats 27), with a few (21) to smaller Communist-linked groupings. Out of the 460 seats, 35 were determined by a 'national list' system, whereby voters could reject candidates by crossing off their names and, if more than 50% did so, the candidate failed to be elected. The constituency seats were determined on the same basis as the Senate – 50% and one on the first round, and a simple majority on the second.

In the first round of the election on 4 June, Solidarity did very well indeed, winning 92 of the 100 Senate seats outright and all but one of the 161 Sejm seats that they were allowed to contest. In many cases their candidates got majorities of 75% and more, well above the 50% plus one needed. The Communists and their allies did very badly, very few candidates being elected outright – only five in all, of whom three had, in fact, the backing of Solidarity. They fared badly too on the national list, despite support from Walesa as well as Jaruzelski, with only two candidates, neither of them Communists, winning through, leaving the others to be determined on the second ballot.

Before the second round on 18 June the humiliated figures on the national list dropped out, leaving 66 new candidates to contend for the 33 seats in supplementary elections. This second ballot attracted a very low turnout indeed, only 25% compared with 62% two weeks earlier, but the remaining seats were filled. It was clear, however, even at this stage, that some of the Communists' allies would in fact vote in the Sejm not with the Party but with Solidarity. Solidarity won seven of the remaining Senate seats, with the eighth going to an independent, ex-Communist businessman, Stoklosa. The elections therefore left Solidarity in a very strong position, having won virtually all the seats open to it, and the Communist Party in an extremely weak position, with allies whose loyalty could by no means be relied upon. Even among the Party deputies themselves, 80 claimed later not to have had the backing of the Party's apparat and indeed some had indirect links with Solidarity and other radical groupings.

Solidarity, under Walesa's leadership, accepted a Party President, and Jaruzelski was very narrowly elected by a combined meeting of the two chambers, the Sejm or lower house (450 seats) and the Senate (100 seats, 99 held by Solidarity). In August General Kiszczak was elected Prime Minister but proved unable to form a government. Solidarity meanwhile detached the formerly allied Peasants' Party (ZSL) and the Democratic Party (SD) from the Communist Party, and so was itself able to form a government which the Communists, after a telephone conversation with Gorbachev, also decided to join. By early September Tadeusz Mazowiecki had formed a predominately non-Communist government, though with four Party ministers, including Defence and the Interior, and with General Jaruzelski, as President, having ultimate responsibility for foreign policy. It was thought that keeping these appointments in Party hands would be a significant constraint on the Mazowiecki government, but this does not seem to have been the case. Concern had also been expressed that *nomenklatura* appointees in government ministries and as factory managers could sabotage a truly reforming government. Again this does not appear to have occurred: a number of nominal Party members in *nomenklatura* posts seem to have demonstrated how shallow their Party commitment was and, as far as can be seen, have worked effectively for the new government.

The improved political situation did not, of course, change the basically disastrous economic situation, although it did make it possible for the government to conclude an agreement at the end of 1989 with the IMF and move decisively in the direction of a market economy. The drastic anti-inflation package which has been arrived at will, inevitably, be unpopular and lead to recession with increased unemployment. Popular support may not hold up if things get visibly worse and worse. Walesa, too, remains outside the government, and is thus potentially able to distance himself from government actions.

Parties

Poland's political taxonomy has to deal with a society which divides in a wide variety of ways. There is a strong division between rural and urban cultures. The former is much more closely identified with Catholicism, but Catholic influence also extends into the urban intellectual community. There is also a division between Marxists, social democrats and liberals. Within the urban community there is a division within the industrial working-class between members of the Solidarity trade unions and the former official unions. Perhaps more important are the divisions between the hard-headed, the realists and the pragmatists, on the one side, and the idealists on the other.

All of this said, even though Poland has had a very energetic political debate, it has engaged in recent years only a minority of the population. Many people now have a sense of alienation from the whole political process, having heard the call of reforms too often and then having seen few results. This is a further challenge to all the political parties. Although the Polish United Workers' Party (PUWP), as the Communist Party was called, remained in power after the imposition of martial law and the repression of Solidarity in

1981, it was still unable to give an acceptable lead to the Polish people. It met the renewed challenge of Solidarity and the grassroots strikes indecisively – the failure to agree on the round-table talks in the autumn and winter of 1988 showed it clinging to power but not making any real moves to solve the country's very serious problems. Rakowski did at one stage say that he thought the Polish people were more interested in what was on their own tables than in the round-table talks, but he was unable to make any impression on inflation and the deep-seated economic problems. Economic success would not have guaranteed any return of support to the Party, but without it it had no chance.

The June 1989 election made the Party's lack of general support clear: it was unable on the first ballot to fill more than a handful of the seats allocated to it, and obtained no seats at all in the Senate. Its 35 names of top leaders on the national list fared no better – and indeed candidates like Rakowski withdrew before the indignity of the second round of voting. Shortly after the election the PUWP's Central Committee met and elected Rakowski Secretary by 171 votes to 41. Not unnaturally there were considerable divisions in the Party, given its calamitous recent history, culminating in the disastrous election defeat. In February 1990 these resulted in its final dissolution and the formation of two rival social-democratic parties, one claiming to be more Marxist than the other.

The size (2.2 million members in the Solidarity Union) and scope of Solidarity has meant comparatively little development up to now of other new parties. However, since within Solidarity there are at least three distinct groupings, it may well contain the seeds of other parties. The initial trade-union element of Solidarity was joined both by Rural Solidarity and by the intellectual groups who offered their advice early on to Walesa and the student movement. With the advent of the Solidarity-led government, this grouping (OKP) can also be viewed as the parliamentary party, as against the trade-union wing. Not only are there these different groupings within Solidarity, but there are also tensions between old and new leaders, the survivors of 1980–1 and those who became involved only in 1988–9. There is the usual division between the cautious pragmatists (of whom Walesa was one in the difficult period leading to the formation of the Mazowiecki government) and the more militant members. The election of General Jaruzelski as a result of a few, mainly senior, Solidarity figures spoiling their ballot papers, or abstaining, so that he obtained the majority needed by one vote, was not acceptable to all Solidarity members. Nor was the way in which candidates were endorsed for the June elections. Here the issue of Church dominance to some extent arose, since humanist and more socialist Solidarity members were at a disadvantage if, for example, they supported the right to abortion.

The Peasants' Party (ZSL), like other allies of the Communist Party, distanced itself from the Communists towards the end. The leader, Malinowski, supported Janicki for Agriculture Minister in the Mazowiecki government as against the incumbent, Olesiak, also a member of the Peasants' Party. Malinowski has since resigned and the party has been renamed the Peasants' Renewal Party. Possibly at some stage Rural Solidarity might see its interests as closer to ZSL's than to those of the urban trade-union part of Solidarity or any development of less devoutly Catholic intellectual groupings within Solidarity.

The Communist Party's other former ally, the Democratic Party (SD), has two ministries, with Janowski as one of the four Deputy Premiers; the other three are Janicki from the ZSL, Kiszczak from the Communist Party (still, as he has been for many years, Interior Minister) and Balcerowicz from Solidarity.

There are several smaller parties outside the old structures and Solidarity. Peace and Freedom has been mentioned earlier, and although it is primarily a pacifist party, it does to some extent fill the role normally held by the Greens elsewhere. There is also a Social-Democratic Party, founded in December 1987, but it was badly split in early 1988, when its then leader, Lipski, resigned after the party had been harassed and infiltrated by the police. Right-wing groups also exist, such as the Confederation for an Independent Poland, founded in 1979, which had a meeting broken up by police on the day the round-table talks started. In February 1989 the re-establishment of the Christian Democrats was announced in the Sejm by Ryszard Bender, who had sat as an independent until then.

However, given the present dominance of Solidarity, it seems unlikely, even if a period of great disillusion sets in, that other groupings will assume much importance. It is far more likely that Solidarity, which can perhaps, not too fancifully, be likened to a national independence movement, will in time break down into constituent interest groups with which other smaller pre-existing parties will coalesce. There are signs that this is already happening

with the formation of factions within OKP, the Solidarity
Parliamentary Party.

HUNGARY

A particular feature of the Hungarian case is the way in which the
Hungarian Socialist Workers' Party (HSWP) has used its 'leading
role' to promote the reforms, not only in the economy but also in the
political field itself, which have entailed its voluntary abandonment
of its monopoly on power. This has not occurred without outside
pressure, but nevertheless it is important to recognize the crucial role
of the reform faction within the Party itself in enabling the process of
'de-Leninization' to proceed surprisingly smoothly, with virtually no
mass mobilization or breakdown in public order.

The strength of the reform faction in the Party is a result of the
decades of Kadar's rule, which was markedly less dogmatic than
elsewhere in Eastern Europe. Kadar appreciated right from the start
that economic reform (which first came onto the agenda of
Hungarian politics in the early 1960s) would require some adjustments in the way the Party exercised its 'leading role'. Correspond-
.ngly, the *nomenklatura* system appears to have been operated with
rather more flexibility and discernment by the Hungarian Party
apparatus for many years.[4] Ideological conformity was not an
absolute requirement for membership, and, particularly during the
1970s, significant numbers of young technocrats were drawn into the
Party. As elsewhere, Party membership was virtually a *sine qua non*
for a successful career, but in Hungary it was not incompatible with
either a high level of expertise or a wide variety of personal political
views. As became clear in the 1980s, many of the younger generation
in the Party leadership had come to hold the sincere conviction that
the Party's power monopoly was unjustifiable and no longer practi-
cable. A particularly energetic reformist faction developed around
Imre Pozsgay. After the removal of Janos Kadar, this group became
embroiled in a power struggle with other, more conservative and
authoritarian leaders (in particular, with Kadar's successor, Karoly
Grosz), which the reformers won by the summer of 1989.

In December 1988, a new government was formed under Miklos
Nemeth, a young Harvard-trained economist who was at first
believed to be a protégé of Grosz. However, he quickly proved his
independence, and has played an important role in furthering

political reform in Hungary. The position of Prime Minister had begun to gather authority when Grosz used it as a springboard for his own campaign for the Party leadership. Nemeth has continued to develop this trend of independence from the Party leadership. When he reorganized and reshuffled his government in March 1989, he was able to assure the Hungarian Parliament, on presenting his proposals, that these had not been approved beforehand by the Party's Politburo, as had been the practice hitherto. Thus the *nomenklatura* system was effectively removed from state appointments. However, the government continues to be dominated by Party members, albeit of the radical reformist wing.

In the summer of 1989, the HSWP entered into discussions with the various opposition parties which had sprung into existence, in order to negotiate a peaceful transition to democracy. The negotiations produced agreement in September on some basic constitutional amendments to guarantee civil liberties and the right to form political parties and a new electoral system, and to establish a new Presidency. Some of the opposition groups, however, were unable to lend their support to the agreement, since they objected to the provision for a directly elected Presidency and felt that key elements of the HSWP's power had been left intact: namely, it did not cover the questions of the Party's property, Party organizations in the workplace, or the Party's own paramilitary organization, the Workers' Guard. The omission of these issues reflected deep division within the HSWP leadership over its strategy in the transition to democracy.

In June 1989, the Central Committee, by now increasingly reformist in persuasion and dissatisfied with Grosz's conservative foot-dragging, set up a new four-man leadership to take charge of an accelerated reform programme. Thus General Secretary Grosz was joined (and overshadowed) by a new Party President, the eminent reform economist Rezso Nyers, Prime Minister Nemeth, and the well-known and very popular politician Imre Pozsgay. It was decided that a thorough reform of the HSWP itself was essential to transform it into a modern, Western-style democratic socialist party which would have some chance of avoiding total defeat in future free elections. To this end, an extraordinary Party congress was convened in early October. The issue of transforming the Party was inevitably bitterly contested, and Nyers saw his role as one of mediating between conservative and radical reformist factions in an effort to avoid a split. He thus put his weight behind a compromise at the congress which involved avoiding the questions of workplace Party organizations and the Workers' Guard. This compromise was in fact not only ineffective but very damaging: the credibility of the Party was sacrificed to no purpose. The conservative factions decided after the congress not to recognize the 'new' Hungarian Socialist Party (HSP) which emerged from it; instead, they re-established the HSWP. Membership of the HSP was only a small fraction of that of the former HSWP, while the revived HSWP claimed fairly large support. Moreover, at its late October session, the Hungarian Parliament passed legislation outlawing workplace Party organizations and disbanding the Workers' Guard.

On 23 October 1989, the Hungarian Parliament approved the constitutional amendments agreed in the summer negotiations, and Hungary was proclaimed a Republic by its acting President, another of the former HSWP's leading reformists, Matyas Szuros. The new Presidency was due to be filled in late November by free elections, but a referendum was called on the basis of an effective campaign by the non-communist radical parties, the Alliance of Free Democrats (AFD) and the Young Democrats (Fidesz), who were opposed to the institution of a directly elected Presidency. As a result of this referendum, the election was delayed, and parliamentary elections are to be held first, on 25 March 1990. This interim period has seen the hitherto sure-footed reform communists of the HSP somewhat shaken as events seem to be slipping from their control. The AFD and Fidesz are deeply suspicious of the reformist leadership, and antagonism was only heightened at the start of 1990, when the AFD obtained evidence from an inside source that the Ministry of the Interior had been continuing to tap the phones of opposition parties. This so-called 'Dunagate' (or 'Danube-gate') scandal was given full coverage in the Hungarian media, and has served to weaken the reputation of the reformist leadership. The Minister of the Interior, a close associate of Pozsgay, was forced to resign. Rapid reform of internal security is now promised.

Parties
Hungary's party system, in contrast to that of Czechoslovakia or East Germany, has been evolving steadily over almost two years, and over the past few months several public opinion polls have been

published. The likely outcome of the election, due on 25 March, is therefore a little clearer here. But none of the parties has anywhere near enough support to govern alone, while the deep antagonisms that exist between the major parties are likely to make the formation of an effective coalition government very difficult.

The main development over the past year has been the steady erosion of the position of the ruling party (formerly the Hungarian Socialist Workers' Party, and since October renamed the Hungarian Socialist Party) despite the prominent role it has played in promoting political reform. Party membership fell from 800,000, reported in May 1988, to 720,000 by the time of the October special congress. The Party leadership at the congress made the fatal mistake of releasing former members of the HSWP from their membership, then inviting them to sign up for the successor party, the HSP, setting a deadline of 30 October. In the event, the vast bulk of the membership simply dropped out, and at the end of October only 30,000 had joined the HSP. By the end of 1989, this had risen to 50,000, but the new HSP President, Rezso Nyers, was seriously embarrassed. Meanwhile, disconsolate hardline conservatives regrouped to re-establish the HSWP, and claim to have gathered about 80,000 supporters. The HSP nevertheless enjoys greater support according to public opinion polls – about 12% as compared with only a few per cent for the HSWP, whose electoral support is not likely much to exceed its claimed membership.

The HSP's main strength lies in its leading members, who are prominent, well-known reformers with substantial experience in government: the Prime Minister, Miklos Nemeth, the economist Rezso Nyers, acting President Matyas Szuros, Foreign Minister Gyula Horn, and Imre Pozsgay, Minister of State in charge of political reform since mid-1988. However, events in neighbouring East European countries and the 'Dunagate' scandal referred to above have contributed to a heightened anti-communist popular mood which has been exploited by the main opposition parties. Moreover, the government is still clearly an HSP government, and, inevitably, the unpopular economic measures which, to his credit, Prime Minister Nemeth has pushed through in the past few months have done little to improve the HSP's standing with the electorate.

One of the two most powerful opposition forces is the Hungarian Democratic Forum (HDF). This started life in September 1987 as a political movement of the cultural intelligentsia, supported, moreover, by Imre Pozsgay. Many of its founder members were part of the cultural establishment, in particular, from 'populist' circles. Many also at first combined participation in the HDF with membership of the HSWP. There was some debate in the movement about whether to become a political party or not. Opponents of this felt that the movement should strive to unify the whole nation, and were unwilling to countenance a direct challenge to the HSWP itself. However, in the course of 1989, when membership grew rapidly to over 30,000 and the political context changed equally rapidly, transformation into a party became accepted as inevitable. Moreover, the 'populist' element was somewhat diluted by the inclusion of many more members of a Western-oriented, Christian-Democratic persuasion.

In attracting members, the HDF benefited greatly from the fact that it was the first alternative to the ruling party to appear on the scene. Public information about it was considerable, after the press (particularly the key newspapers connected with Pozsgay's cultural circle) freed itself from the rigidities of HSWP censorship. It has been successful not only among the Budapest cultural intelligentsia but also in the provinces and among the local 'notables' and professional middle classes. The latest public opinion polls indicate that over 20% of voters are likely to opt for it in an election, the largest support for any party. Its main programme is both democratic and nationalist, with a Christian flavour. On the question of economic reform, it professes commitment to a 'social market' economy. Its leaders no doubt are fully aware of the necessity of radical economic reform, but the populist tendency within the HDF has been ready to exploit dissatisfaction with certain inevitable concomitants of economic reform, such as rising prices. Occasionally its representatives have been heard to express misgivings about the sale of national assets to foreigners, which may indicate some ambiguity in its commitment to opening up the economy to the world market. There is also an undercurrent of anti-semitism in the party, which is the source of antagonism in its relationship with the other major opposition party, the Alliance of Free Democrats (AFD).

The origins of the AFD are to be found in the small 'Democratic Opposition' underground movement of Budapest intellectuals, active from the late 1970s onwards. When the AFD was established in late 1988, it attracted fresh support from some of the leading specialist economists who had been responsible for most of the economic reform programme for many years. The frustration of these members of the elite with the performance of the HSWP leadership and the government reached a point in the mid-1980s where they no longer believed in the possibility of implementing a coherent reform programme through the existing political structures, and they therefore developed links with the democratic opposition.

The AFD programme, as a result, is by far the most convincing, coherent statement of a reform policy available, and has in fact influenced all the other parties' programmes. The task for the AFD has been to build up its mass support, in order to throw off its image of a narrow group of the Budapest intellectual elite. It is developing its appeal as a secular party, embracing political tendencies from left-of-centre to right-of-centre, but all firmly committed to the fundamental liberal principles of individual freedom, human rights, pluralist democracy and the market economy. It is rather wary of Hungarian nationalism and resolutely rejects the idea of a 'third road' between capitalism and communism (which sometimes surfaces in HDF thinking). Instead, it prefers to emphasize the 'Western' elements of Hungary's cultural identity, and is fully committed to securing the country's closest possible political and economic integration with Western Europe.

Public opinion polls show that the AFD's support has risen rapidly, from only about 5% in the summer of 1989 to over 20% by the early spring of 1990. There are many links and overlaps between the AFD and the Young Democrats, or Fidesz, which has been gathering a following among young people (winning about 6–7% support in opinion polls). Fidesz has a rather flamboyant radicalism which attracts much public attention, although occasionally it may put off the more cautious among the electorate.

Two further parties are revivals from the pre-communist period, both of which may be prepared to work in coalition with the AFD and Fidesz (the four parties worked together in the November 1989 referendum, against both the HSP and the HDF). The first is the Social-Democratic Party, which emerged early in 1989 as a strong challenger to the HSWP, but subsequently lost public confidence as a result of some protracted and bitter in-fighting. Its opinion poll support had fallen to 4–5% at the beginning of 1990. The second of the so-called 'historic' parties is the Independent Smallholders'

Party, which was in fact by far the largest party in 1945, in Hungary's last free elections. It may draw support from the same professional and middle-class groups as the HDF, but it is more strongly anti-communist and more firmly committed to liberal, free-market economics. It should therefore be attractive to the small but rapidly growing class of private entrepreneurs as well as the self-employed. It also enjoys relatively large support in rural areas, and is in direct competition with the HDF in this respect. Opinion polls indicate that its support grew rapidly in the autumn of 1989 to about 10% of those polled, and rose further to over 16% in January 1990. Its support also appears to be the firmest of any of the major parties (85% say they are sure to support it in the March elections, as compared with an average of 66% for all parties).

An important characteristic of the Hungarian situation is the high level of public apathy about politics. There was a series of parliamentary by-elections in the second half of 1989, at which turnout was very low, in some cases less than 50%, which thus forced a repeat ballot. This reflects a rather widespread resignation and fatalism: people are most worried about the dire state of the economy, and they (rightly) recognize that none of the parties has an instant solution. The opinion polls indicate not only that none of the parties enjoys a great deal of support, but also a high degree of uncertainty (at least 25% 'don't know') and a rather weak level of commitment to any party (only two-thirds of those who indicated a definite choice of party in December were sure they would not change their minds by the time of the March 1990 elections). There is a deep scepticism about the value of political participation, which is worrying, since it could lead to a rather low level of acceptance of the next, democratically accountable, government. There is thus a lingering fear of the rise of a demagogic anti-reform backlash. The danger of this should not, at present, be exaggerated.

CZECHOSLOVAKIA

After twenty years of remarkably thoroughgoing and ruthless 'normalization' following the Prague Spring of 1968 (which in many ways provided a prototype of Gorbachev's *perestroika*),[5] communist power collapsed remarkably quickly in Czechoslovakia. The immediate cause of this was a series of massive popular demonstrations in late November 1989, initially provoked by outrage at the brutal methods used by the police to disperse a peaceful student rally. The crisis was not only sudden but peaceful, thanks largely to the rapid emergence of an effective non-communist organization, the Civic Forum, which grouped together numerous small oppositional groups and the representatives of the students and theatre workers who played a key role as a catalyst of the mass movement. The Communist Party leadership under Milos Jakes, a hardliner and reputedly ruthless politician, is believed to have considered the use of armed force to repress the wave of demonstrations, but failed to secure the support of the Central Committee, and so stepped down.

The new Presidium of the Party, elected at a crisis session of the Central Committee, still contained many old faces. This reluctance of the top Party bodies to face up to the situation precipitated a crisis of confidence among the rank-and-file membership, and also drew open criticism from the Prime Minister, Ladislav Adamec, who rapidly recognized the unavoidability of conducting dialogue with the opposition Civic Forum and its Slovak counterpart, Public Against Violence, many of whose leading figures had long suffered police harassment and imprisonment for their human rights activities. Adamec opened round-table discussions with the opposition, and promised to form a new government containing non-communists. In the event, he disappointed both the opposition and the Czechoslovak public as a whole by forming a government containing fifteen communists out of the total twenty-one members. The non-communists, moreover, did not enjoy the full support of the opposition.

After a renewed wave of massive public demonstrations and the threat of a general strike, Adamec was forced to quit and another new government was formed under the Slovak Marian Calfa, formerly senior legal adviser to the Czechoslovak government and, at this time, a Communist Party member. The government included eight Party members, who were joined by thirteen non-communists: nine unaffiliated members and two each from the Socialist Party and People's Party. The new team was approved by the opposition. Four of the communists – the Prime Minister himself, two top economic experts, First Deputy Prime Minister Valtr Komarek and the new Planning Commission head, Vladimir Dlouhy, and the Prime Minister of Slovakia, Milan Cic – have since resigned from the Party. The President, Gustav Husak, whose name was inseparably linked in the public mind with the dismal period of 'normalization' after 1968, swore in the Calfa government and then tendered his own resignation. Czechoslovakia is a federal state, with national governments in the Czech Lands (the provinces of Bohemia and Moravia) and in Slovakia; similarly composed 'governments of national understanding' were established at this level too. Finally, on 29 December, the National Assembly (Parliament) elected the leading figure in the Civic Forum, playwright and long-time opposition activist Vaclav Havel, as President of the Republic.

Therefore, at the level of top leadership, Czechoslovakia has gone further than any of its neighbours in removing communist control. Both the President and the government consider themselves to be transitional: free elections are to be held on 8 June 1990. Meanwhile, the government is taking vigorous legislative action to satisfy popular demand for democratic political reform, and the Communist Party has not used its control over the majority in the National Assembly to block change; in fact, large numbers of communist deputies resigned and the Party announced it would ask others to follow suit, to make way for representatives of the new political movements, so relinquishing the communist majority in all representative bodies. The National Assembly passed a constitutional amendment removing the reference to the 'leading role of the Communist Party', outlawed party organizations in workplaces and dropped the word 'Socialist' from the name of the Czechoslovak Republic. One of the two First Deputy Prime Ministers, the Slovak Catholic human rights activist and lawyer, Jan Carnogursky, has been put in charge of constitutional reforms in the area of human rights and civil liberties. The Minister of the Interior, Richard Sacher, a non-communist, has taken on the task of reform of the security police, whose internal surveillance functions have been abolished, and whose other functions are to be transferred to the regular police.

Substantial spontaneous turnover of personnel has been going on throughout the apparatus at lower levels, with the resignation or firing of *nomenklatura* political appointees. The Communist Party itself has reduced the size of its apparatus by over 80% to a total staff of 2,082, of which 198 form the Central Committee apparatus. The Party press contains complaints of 'victimization' of communists who have allegedly been unjustly fired, or who are unable to find new jobs on account of their Party membership. Membership has been falling rapidly (see below), which is not surprising now that

27

the major reason for joining, the *nomenklatura* system, has collapsed. The Prime Minister remains firm on the need to part company with those political appointees who are incompetent, unpopular and lacking in credibility, while President Havel and other Civic Forum leaders have shown impressive concern that justice should be observed in each case of dismissal. They warn against repeating the indiscriminate mass sackings of experienced professional cadres which took place under the communists after 1948 and again after 1968. This is recognized as economically damaging, particularly in the case of enterprise management. President Havel is also, characteristically, deeply concerned with the moral aspects of this issue, and is a passionate advocate of the values of toleration and generosity of spirit which are essential to rebuilding a social environment in which open, democratic politics can develop. Thus the difficult process of 'de-Leninization' appears to be progressing as well as could be hoped for anywhere.

Parties
In Czechoslovakia, and particularly in the Czech Lands, there is a long tradition, dating well back into the nineteenth century, of active participation in clubs, societies and voluntary associations of all kinds. This tradition has not been completely extinguished in the past forty years, and the rapid emergence of a lively, pluralistic 'civil society' can be expected. The main division in the political culture runs along national lines, between Czechs and Slovaks. The Czech Lands, with an industrial tradition dating back to the nineteenth century and thus a long-established working-class movement, are characterized by a mainly secular, egalitarian and socialistic political culture, while in more rural Slovakia, Catholic conservatism is a powerful force. The strength of socialist ideology has no doubt been very much weakened by the experience of recent decades, and indeed there is some evidence of enthusiasm for private enterprise: a new Association for Private Entrepreneurs, set up recently to offer advice to would-be new entrants to this field, reports that it received 50,000 requests for information in the first fortnight of its existence. Tensions between the two very different national cultures have, in the past, proved fatefully damaging to Czechoslovak politics, and a major task for new parties will be to attempt to integrate the two parts of the Republic.

Let us begin by assessing the prospects for survival under democratic conditions of the Communist Party (CPCS) and its associated 'block parties'. The CPCS had 1.7 million members before the November 1989 crisis. No reliable reports have emerged on its current size: the CPCS itself claims to have lost 200,000 members, but this could well be an underestimate. The main attraction of Party membership after 1968 was to further one's career prospects. This has now disappeared. However, a group of genuine reform communists, the Democratic Forum of Communists, has sprung up among some rank-and-file enthusiasts, claiming 60,000 adherents. Although it is technically a 'fraction' (or factional grouping), thus contravening Party rules, it is tolerated by the new CPCS leadership under Ladislav Adamec (CPCS President) and Vasil Mohorita (General Secretary), who are both well aware of the Party's poor electoral prospects and the need to transform its image into a more open, internally variegated one. However, the Democratic Forum of Communists seems likely to transform itself into a separate party in the near future, thereby furthering the weakening and disintegration of the left wing of the political spectrum. It is also conducting talks with the 'Obroda' (Revival) group of former CPCS members, expelled after 1968. These include several ministers from the 1968 Dubcek government. It is indicative of the CPCS's sense of its own rootedness in Czechoslovak culture that it continues to describe itself openly as 'communist', in contrast, for example, to the Hungarian and Polish parties, which have tried to resuscitate their credibility by renaming themselves 'socialist' or 'social-democratic'. However, the CPCS cannot rely on the traditional high level of support for leftist parties, given its poor record. Electoral support in June is likely to be very low.

The CPCS did not outlaw all other parties after 1948, but kept on four of them in a largely ineffective coalition formation, the 'National Front'. Two of these parties, however, have shown some signs of life in the recent months. This is particularly true of the Czechoslovak Socialist Party, which played a very important role in the November crisis, offering facilities to the opposition Civic Forum and acting as an initial bridge between it and the government. It has changed its leadership and is now better prepared to put itself forward as the legitimate descendant of Tomas Masaryk's National Socialists. Masaryk is an important symbol (although more so for Czechs than for Slovaks) of the democratic, progressive political values of Czechoslovakia's pre-communist past. The Slovak People's Party has re-emerged as a force representing Catholic interests and views, and is engaged in discussions with former underground opposition Catholic activists with a view to forming a Christian-Democratic type of party which could gather votes in both Slovakia and the Czech Lands. The electorate in the latter, however, is still largely secular.

The re-establishment of a Social-Democratic Party could have drawn enormous support among the electorate, but, as elsewhere in Eastern Europe, Social Democrats have become deeply divided on various points of principle and personality, which is likely to undermine voters' confidence. A Green Party has sprung up, which claims a huge (but unverifiable) membership. There is no doubt that, given the severity of the environmental problems of the country (which is probably the most polluted in Europe), environmental issues will be at the forefront of voters' minds when they make their choices in June. Moreover, the rather unorthodox nature of the Green Party may appeal to voters tired of rigidly organized, traditional party structures. This brings us on to the key opposition organization, the Civic Forum.

The origins of the Civic Forum lie in the Charter 77 human rights movement. In November 1989, the Forum was quickly set up by Vaclav Havel to unite all the various opposition groups. It is an umbrella movement, containing various different groupings, ideologies and objectives, and it therefore lacks the coherence of a political party; it is not clear that it intends to become one either. Its main roles to date have been to unite the opposition to communist rule, to negotiate with the old leadership as a self-appointed representative of the whole people, and to supply nominees for the new government. It derives its legitimacy directly from the popular revolt of November-December 1989, and its authority has been greatly enhanced by the personal role of Vaclav Havel. Although some of the new parties which have sprung up have emerged from under the wing of the Civic Forum, the latter does intend to put up its own candidates at the next election. The thinking behind this is that the Civic Forum can play a more useful role, at least in the short term, in coordinating a common platform among the great number of embryonic new parties which are still numerically small and may be unable to gather the 10,000 signatures that the new law on political parties requires before a party can participate in elections.

Moreover, President Havel has expressed concern that individuals of ability but without firm party commitment should be able to stand for election, and the Civic Forum might endorse such candidates. It is also appreciated that the public may not readily trust traditional types of parties and would prefer a looser, less formal movement representing a few basic principles (democracy, human rights), at least until the general situation becomes clearer.

The proposed electoral system of proportional representation by party lists will certainly prove more effective if the Civic Forum pursues this integrating strategy. The country is divided into twelve large multi-member constituencies, whose deputies will be allocated to the parties according to their share of the vote. Deputies' names will be drawn from lists supplied by the parties themselves. No party will be allocated seats unless it wins at least 5% of the total vote in either the Czech Lands or Slovakia as a whole. The latter provision is designed to limit the proliferation of parties, which is a necessary safeguard: at least 36 parties are reported to have applied to register legally so far.

The election is thus likely to produce a highly variegated Parliament, but fortunately the stability of the government does not depend on firm party discipline to the extent that it does in, say, British politics. The government is appointed by the President, subject to parliamentary approval. Despite the variety of political forces emerging, there is a substantial degree of common ground on the basic tasks facing the country.

The post of President will become very much more important. Czechoslovakia has been uniquely fortunate in the person of Vaclav Havel, and, although he originally made it clear that he took on the post only as an interim, transitional measure, it is likely that he will be persuaded to stand once again for a full term, before he is allowed to return to his preferred vocation of playwright.[6]

GDR

The GDR differs in one very important respect from all the other East European countries in that its entire population has the possibility of emigrating to the West, whereas in other countries this is an option only for ethnic Germans and Jews.[7]

As long as migration was effectively prevented, East Germany could maintain one of the more efficient communist systems; once this control had become impossible because of the opening of Hungary's border to Austria in August 1989 the whole situation became unstable. Things then moved very rapidly. Although there had been mumblings of dissatisfaction over the alleged rigging of local election ballots in May 1989, with a hundred people arrested in Leipzig, the first serious pressure was put on the regime in August, when would-be refugees poured into the West German mission in East Berlin and their embassies in Budapest, Prague and Warsaw. From then on the pressure from migration intensified. By the end of September 1989 it was being estimated that over 100,000, mainly young and skilled, would have left by the end of the year. This migration, and most importantly its effect on the economy, are one of the main destabilizing factors in East Germany.

As the migration flow built up, so did the internal protest. Erich Honecker, the East German leader, was in poor health, and the Politburo was dominated by aged hardliners, one of whom, Hermann Axen, described East Germany as late as mid-September as 'a bulwark of socialism and peace in the heart of Europe'. During September demonstrations started and the Protestant Church called for consultation about the country's problems. The Protestant Church played a most important role in providing a secure space in which political discussion could be held. Most demonstrations started from churches – the St Nicholas Church in Leipzig and the Gethsemane Church in East Berlin being particularly important. Early in September there was an open meeting of New Forum, then a small group of intellectuals and Protestant clergymen. Their first declaration was signed by 25 people calling on all to join in debate, since 'communication between state and society in our country has broken down'. A few days later, on Sunday 17 September, an appeal for dialogue was made from all Protestant pulpits.

The authorities' first reaction was to clamp down on protest. One hundred people were taken into custody at a demonstration in Leipzig, and four of them were very quickly sentenced to four months in gaol for riotous assembly. New Forum asked in vain for legal registration. Signs of independence of two of the 'block' parties – the Liberal Democrats (LDPD) and the Christian Democrats (CDUD) – were ignored. The Catholic bishops also expressed disquiet, but to no effect.

Migration and demonstrations continued, and it was against this background that the 40th-anniversary celebrations of the GDR were held, with Honecker escorting Gorbachev to official events on 7 October while the demonstrators elsewhere were using 'Gorbi' as one of their slogans in calling for change. Gorbachev made it quite clear that the solution to East Germany's problems lay in Berlin, not Moscow.

Shortly after Gorbachev left, the first reports of splits in the Politburo appeared. Demonstrators were released and dialogue was offered in Leipzig and Dresden by the local Communist Party (SED) leaders. The regime made its first cautious statements about being open for discussion but it was already too late – the popular forces were in full swing. It became clear, too, that opposition and the desire for change were no longer confined to intellectuals and the middle class, but were affecting industrial workers. Tisch, the trade-union leader, and other Politburo members visited factories and found the situation 'very tense'. On Saturday 14 October, New Forum held a coordinating meeting of 120 people and claimed the support of 25,000. Two days later (on 16 October) the regular Monday demonstration in Leipzig was attended by over 100,000 people, and the slogan 'The Wall Must Go' was seen.

The official media became more open about the situation, which rapidly deteriorated from the government's point of view. By this time 34,139 East Germans had left for the West via Hungary. On 18 October Honecker resigned and was succeeded by Egon Krenz. Krenz immediately went to the large 7 October factory in Berlin to meet workers, and also met Party and trade-union officials and Bishop Leich. On 20 October travel was freed completely – all having the right to a passport and to apply for a visa. Appeals were made to those who had left to return. Demonstrations, however, continued and spread; for the first time there was one in the north, at Rostock, attended by over 10,000 people.

On 24 October Krenz was duly elected as President by the Volkskammer – the Parliament – but with an unprecedented 26 votes against and 26 abstentions. In East Berlin a few days later the local Party leader, Günther Schabowski, met Jens Reich and Sebastian Pflugbeil, two of New Forum's leaders. At the end of the month there was an amnesty for peaceful demonstrators. Demonstrations continued to grow in size – on 30 October, 300,000 marched in Leipzig.

Concessions by the regime continued. Krenz promised proposals for change before the 1991 elections. All, however, was far too little, too late. Resignations began – first Tisch, then Margot Honecker,

Bernd Seidel, the mayor of Leipzig, and five elderly members of the Politburo. On the first weekend in November a demonstration in Berlin was claimed to involve nearly a million people, or 6% of the country's entire population.

A new Politburo was formed on 8 November, consisting of eleven members, of whom Krenz was the youngest at 52. The Wall was opened and people poured through to look at West Berlin. A special Party conference was called for 15–17 December and New Forum was legalized. In the first six days after the opening of the Wall, about half the population obtained visas to visit the West. In all, 7,765,881 visas were issued, and in the same six-day period 13,579 emigration requests were approved. Change continued, with Modrow becoming Prime Minister and a new, smaller, government being set up, in which the increasingly independent block parties had 11 out of the 27 posts. Revelations began of corruption and luxury in high places, which aroused great resentment. Unification became prominent on the national agenda – on 11 November it was reported that the weekly poll by the Wickert Institute of Tübingen had found 67% of their sample of 1490 East Germans in favour of reunification, as compared with 59% the previous week. Support for the SED had fallen from 17% to 14%.

Round-table talks were scheduled by the government for 7 December, with two representatives from each of 7 new independent parties, 14 for the 5 parties in the Volkskammer and 3 representatives of the Churches. Krenz said he would scrap the constitutional provision for the leading role of the SED, and this was duly done by the Volkskammer on 1 December, with 5 abstainers and no dissenters. However, a motion to remove the constitutional provision that the country was 'a socialist state of farmers and workers' failed, although it did attract 112 votes from the 500-seat Chamber.

Krenz and the Politburo resigned on 3 December, after only three weeks in office. Dates were advanced both for the elections (6 May instead of 1991) and for the SED congress (9–10 December instead of 17–18 December). At the Party congress, Gregor Gysi, a reforming lawyer, was elected as Party leader, with Modrow as one of his deputies.

Arrests of the old leaders were made, corruption inquiries into 200 people instigated and the Stasi (the security police) officially dissolved. Demonstrations continued, and worrying signs appeared of some extreme right-wing elements. There was violence against Stasi offices, some being occupied.

The beginning of 1990 saw a thoroughly unstable situation, in which the election date was yet again advanced – to 18 March. By early February there was every indication that this would be won outright by Social Democrats (SPD), only formed in October 1989. Unification seemed ever nearer, being made more and more necessary by the collapse of the economy, the continued migration and the popular withdrawal of consent from the government. The prospect of unification has reopened the debate over the security arrangements for a unified Germany. Gorbachev's call for neutrality, which was rebuffed by the present West German leadership, has greater resonance with the majority of the political parties in East Germany and in parts of West Germany's SPD. The decision to offer a common currency, taken by the Federal government on 8 February 1990, with the reluctant support of the Bundesbank, was made on the basis of a balance of evils – a currency union being seen as the least bad option to slow the flow of migrants from East Germany, then reported to be running at up to 3,000 a day.

Parties
The old East German Socialist Unity Party, the SED, had been based on a forced merger of the CP and the SDP in the immediate postwar period – symbolized by joined hands (now removed) on the front of the Party headquarters. There were in addition four 'block' parties – the Christian Democrats (CDUD), the Farmers', or Peasants', Party, the Liberal Democrats (LDPD) and the National Democrats. Though originally subservient to the SED, once unrest developed the LDPD, in particular, showed increasing independence. The newspapers owned by the block parties, each having a national paper as well as local ones, promoted freer discussion earlier than the Communist-owned papers in the period of rapid change. Each party had a membership of 100,000 or rather more.

The first new independent group to be established was New Forum, whose first meeting, held on 12 September, issued a founding declaration signed by 25 people. In addition to Jens Reich and Sebastian Pflugbeil, its early leaders included the painter Bärbel Bohley, the former communist and later dissident Rolf Heinrich and the head of Magdeburg Evangelical Academy, Hans-Jochen

Tschiche. Support for New Forum grew quickly. About a fortnight after its foundation it was claimed that 3,000 people had signed its declaration. By the time of its first large coordination meeting on 14 October, attended by 120 people, the support of 25,000 was claimed by Sebastian Pflugbeil. By the end of October, 100,000 were said to have signed the founding declaration, though New Forum lacked the means to circulate information to them. Contacts were made by New Forum with the Alternative List – the radical Greens – in West Berlin. New Forum, however, suffered from uncertainty about its role – was it an umbrella organization or a political party? It decided to fight the elections, but not as a political party. Within New Forum there are different strands of opinion. Some, like Bohley and Lutz Nagorski, one of the East Berlin leaders, clearly want a socialist society, though of a quite different kind from the failed state socialism of the past, and are against reunification. Others, however, feel differently, as is shown by a statement early in December by Claus Gerd Scheidig and Christiane Paetzold, urging a quick referendum on reunification, since it was no longer 'an unthinkable utopia'. Although New Forum made much of the early running and went to the Round Table on 7 December with about 200,000 supporters, well in excess of the number claimed by any of the other six participants, it has lost standing since. An opinion poll published on 7 February gave it only 4% support, running a poor fourth.

At the time of the allocation of seats for the 7 December Round Table the six independent parties that were represented in addition to New Forum were: Democracy Now, Democratic Awakening, the Social Democrats, the Free Democrats, the Greens and the United Left. The February poll mentioned above gives a very different picture: it shows the SPD with 54%, the Party of Democratic Socialism (the latest name of the old SED or ruling Communist Party) with 12% and the CDU with 11%. The former 'block' party, the Liberal Democratic Party, got 3%. No other party polled as much as 3%.

The SPD was mooted early in September and was formally founded on 7 October (the 40th anniversary of the GDR) at a very small meeting at the flat of Pastor Joachim Kähler at Schwante, near Berlin. The original SPD having completely lost its identity in the SED, the new SPD can – and does – claim to be a completely fresh party. It has grown rapidly and, now travel is free and the Wall is down, has developed strong links with the West German SPD. West

German constituencies have adopted East German ones, and have helped materially and organizationally. The Party now claims 100,000 members under its leader, Ibrahim Böhme. Historically, parts of East Germany, especially Saxony, were among the strongest SPD areas, and this tradition – plus familiarity from television with the West German SPD – has helped its growth.

The Party of Democratic Socialism (previously SED) retains a block of support. Its surviving members must be convinced communists, since for opportunists it is no longer of any use. Its membership, which in early 1989 was getting on for 3 million out of a population of 16 million, had fallen to 900,000 by February 1990.

Like the West German SPD, the West German CDU has also formed links with East German parties and now supports the Alliance for Germany. This was formed at the beginning of February 1990 and comprises the CDU, Democratic Awakening and the German Social Union. The East German CDU is one of the old block parties with a change of leadership, and the other two are new parties. Democratic Awakening was formed at the end of September 1989, at a small meeting much hampered by the police and by travel bans. Its founders were, for the most part, intellectuals and clergymen. By the start of the round-table discussions it had about 6,000 members. The German Social Union was formed later, under the leadership of Wolfgang Schnur, and has links with the Bavarian CSU. Its founding conference, held in Leipzig in mid-December, was attended by 300 delegates, including West German CDU politicians. It called for an end to the division of Europe and a free market economy with social and ecological emphases.

The West German Free Democrats are allied with the most adventurous of the block parties, the Liberal Democrats (LDPD) and the newly formed Free Democratic Party (FDP). The links with the LDPD go back to the pre-reform period, and the LDPD did join the reform process relatively early, but the FDP has had doubts about their commitment to reform.

A left-wing alliance has also been formed for the elections: Alliance 90, which consists of New Forum, Democracy Now and the Initiative for Peace and Human Rights. Democracy Now was one of the first three new parties to be formed and had seats at the Round Table. It was formed mainly by Christians and critical Marxists. Among its leaders is a physicist named Fischbeck. Its aim is democratic and open socialism.

In terms of political parties, as in all others, the future for East Germany is increasingly a German future. In a new German state, which cannot long be delayed, the GDR will form five *Länder*. Even without formal unification, what happens in East Germany is likely to have repercussions for the West German elections due later this year. Just as West German politicians have appeared on East German platforms – Chancellor Kohl, for example, made six electoral appearances – East Germans will appear in the West. Though the East German government tried to stop East and West German politicians appearing on platforms together, this, like most of their recent efforts, has proved futile.

The results of the election on 18 March showed a clear majority in favour of speedy unification, with nearly half the votes going to the centre-right Alliance for Germany, mainly to the CDU. It now seems likely that monetary union will follow shortly, as will discussions on the issue of political union.

This may be achieved by the establishment of five *Länder*, and, following elections in each of them in May, each could apply to join the Federal Republic directly under Article 23 of the Federal Republic's constitution. The alternative of some form of confederation, moving by stages to a federation, would presumably take longer as constitutional agreements would have to be drawn up.

In either case, any agreement between the two German states has to be put to the four powers under the two-plus-four agreement reached in Ottawa in February. In turn this is to be considered by the CSCE meeting planned for the autumn of 1990. If the Article 23 route is followed, the question of GDR membership of the EC will not arise; if the form of confederation is adopted, an application will have to be considered before the end of 1990. The question of the security relationships of the enlarged Germany is not yet resolved: it involves not only the question of whether the united country should be a member of NATO or maintain a neutral position, and the future of Soviet and Western forces stationed in Germany, but also the East German armed forces, which include the second most powerful navy in the Warsaw Pact.

Notes

1 See J. Hough, *The Soviet Prefects* (Cambridge, MA, and London: Oxford University Press, 1969).

2 For an account of political resistance to reform in past Hungarian

and Czechoslovak reform attempts, see J. Batt, *Economic Reform and Political Change in Eastern Europe* (London: Macmillan, 1988).

3 On recent Polish history, see N. Ascherson, *The Polish August* (Harmondsworth, Middlesex: Penguin, 1981); and T. Garton Ash, *The Polish Revolution: Solidarity 1980–82* (London: Cape, 1982).

4 See Batt, op. cit.

5 On recent Czechoslovak history, see H.G. Skilling, *Czechoslovakia's Interrupted Revolution* (Princeton and Guildford: Princeton University Press, 1976); and V. Kusin, *From Dubcek to Charta 77* (Edinburgh: Q Press, 1978).

6 For examples of the political thinking of Havel and other leading Czech and Slovak oppositionists, see V. Havel, *The Power of the Powerless* (London: Hutchinson, 1986).

7 For a general account of GDR politics and society, see M. Dennis, *The German Democratic Republic* (London: Pinter, 1988).

3
THE ECONOMIC PROBLEM

J.M.C. Rollo and Brigitte Granville

> 'Where there is no free market, there is no pricing mechanism;
> without a pricing mechanism, there is no economic calculation.'
> LUDWIG VON MISES

The economic diversity of the East European countries is striking. They have different resources, production methods and trade patterns. Their economies have followed different policy paths over the past twenty years, which have resulted in different sets of short-term problems, both microeconomic and macroeconomic in nature.

The problems
The common feature of these economies is a legacy of Leninist economic structures. Broadly speaking, that legacy is one of centralized resource allocation, monopolistic production structures, autarkic trade policy, non-convertible currencies and a widespread use of subsidies. The result has been a distortion of the price of goods, services and the factors of production, labour and capital. The environment has also suffered as a result of the Leninist approach to resource management.

The micro economy
The primary structural problem facing all these economies at the end of the 1980s was price distortion. The prices of goods and factors of production did not reflect the true cost of the resources used. As a

result there were surpluses of some goods and extreme scarcity of others. The depth and pervasiveness of these distortions is difficult to exaggerate. Food was cheap but in shortage. A great deal of time and energy was spent searching out and queueing for basic goods. The cost to the economy was substantial. Consumer durables were relatively expensive and in short supply. There were none the less long waiting-lists for these durables, fuelled by the accumulated savings of people with nothing else to spend cash on.

Ideology, the requirements of the military and the impact of monopolistic firms and trade unions on the bureaucratic process and on restrictive trade regimes deformed the structure of output. Investment was favoured at the expense of consumption. Quantity – meeting the plan target – was favoured at the expense of quality. The provision of goods was given much higher priority than the provision of services.

The power of the planners lay in their command over capital and its allocation. As well as its direct impact on patterns of production and investment, this bureaucratic control had indirect but none the less important effects. Above all, the absence of a commercial banking system or other means of bringing together entrepreneurs and investors contributed to the lack of innovation and adaptation in the East European economies.

The other factor which suppressed innovation and flexibility was a monopolistic industrial structure, backed by autarkic trade regimes. This allowed the continued production of high-price/poor-quality goods which were uncompetitive on world markets and often unwanted on home markets. These tendencies were intensified by two interrelated issues: the labour market and the absence of a binding income constraint on firms.

Labour market problems derived to a large extent from the fact that in the socialized sectors of the economy in Eastern Europe it was extremely difficult to redeploy workers. This situation had come about partly as a result of legal provisions, and partly because of the political power of trade unions and party cells in factories and workers' councils. The absence of unemployment insurance indicates the extent to which labour immobility was considered a part of the system. As well as its impact on production costs and efficiency, the immobility of the labour market had longer-term effects. Individuals had no incentive to continue training, seek better jobs or improve themselves through training in new skills. As a result, flexibility was restricted and opportunities for innovation lost.

As for the second issue, the lack of a binding income constraint on firms – or the 'soft budget constraint', as it has come to be called (after Kornai) – this is a concept familiar to British and other West European taxpayers who have been faced with the bill for losses on public-sector monopolies (e.g. the railways). Such losses result in part from government-imposed pricing policies. They do, however, contain an element of excess costs that derives from inefficient production structures. Costs are often above the level likely in an equivalent private monopoly. The inability to go bankrupt, whether for legal or for political reasons, relieves state enterprises of the minor constraint (for a monopoly) of controlling costs in the pursuit of profit. The managers and workforce in such regimes are under no discipline apart from the quantitative production target.

The macro economy

Distortions at the level of the market clearly also affect the management of the economy as a whole. State spending in Eastern Europe has been much larger proportionally than anything found in the West. It was funded largely by taxes on spending and on profits, and was used mainly to fund subsidies to consumers and to firms. Further, it has been the tradition in socialist countries for budgets to be balanced. However, it would seem that the tradition of the balanced budget died out in the 1980s (ECE, 1989, pp. 113–15). Tradition lapsed for a number of reasons. The increased aspirations of East European consumers, and the consequent political unrest, led to subsidies being raised without a corresponding increase in taxation taking place – a state of affairs which produced severe budgetary constraints. The absence of domestic capital markets, and hence the inability of the government to raise non-inflationary bond finance, led to the consequent deficit being monetized or funded by increased foreign borrowing. Result: repressed inflation. The symptoms of this repressed inflation were different in different places. They included the rise of black markets for goods and foreign currency, long waiting-lists for consumer durables, the need to export all available goods in order to service debt, large unspent cash balances in banks and under mattresses – the so-called monetary overhang – and large current-account deficits on the balance of payments which could be corrected only by deep and potentially inflationary depreciation of the currency.

Table 3.1 Air pollution indicators, 1985
(kg produced per year per head)

Pollutant	Poland	Hungary	Czecho-slovakia	GDR	FRG
Sulphur oxides	115	131	203	n.a.	52
Suspended particulate matter	65	46	88	n.a.	12
Nitrous oxides	5	37	72	n.a.	49

Source: 'Environment Statistics in Europe and North America: An Experimental Compendium', *Statistical Standards and Studies*, no. 39 (UN Economic Commission for Europe, 1987).

In some cases the repressed inflation broke through. At the end of 1989 Poland and Yugoslavia faced the prospect of hyperinflation. The official rate in Hungary was around 20%. But in the other countries official inflation remained very low. This is perhaps believable in Czechoslovakia, which does seem to have followed prudent fiscal and monetary policies in the years since 1968. East Germany is a special case, and has become more so as open borders and the *de facto* convertibility of the East German mark have begun to take effect.

The environment
The failures of economic policy in Eastern Europe have contributed directly to environmental degradation. The market may not deal well with all aspects of environmental conservation, but non-market systems do even less well – perhaps catastrophically less well.

Poor performance has not been due to a failure to set environmental standards; standards were in fact set at high levels. The core of the problem was lack of competition, and a lack of discipline among producers to control costs, which led to waste of materials and energy. The protection afforded to firms by the bureaucracy also undermined whatever legal responsibility the firms may technically have had. A major contributing factor was the need to use brown coal, with its high sulphur content and low calorific value (see Table 3.1).

The policy response
Having discussed the underlying problems in general terms, we now need to consider the required responses in equally general terms

before turning to the circumstances in the individual countries. As noted in Chapter 2 and above, the question for Eastern Europe is what to replace Leninist structures with and how.

Previous reforms have failed largely because change in goods markets alone was not enough. Power over essential allocative decisions remained with the central institutions of party and state. The simple answer is to take that power away from the central institutions and give it back to individuals and firms. The market is the obvious solution. But, like an elephant, a market economy is difficult to define, even if most people recognize one when they see one. The range of state involvement in what are recognizably market economies is wide, with the Nordic countries and Austria at one end of the spectrum and the USA at the other.

So what are the essential features? The existence of an open pricing system is certainly one: that is, a system where prices are set by willing buyers and willing sellers. By itself, however, that is not enough, hence the failure of past price reform when applied on its own.

Second, if an enterprise is to operate efficiently, there must be in place a system of incentives which allocates ultimate control of resources to a person or entity whose economic well-being depends on the efficient management of those resources. The sanction on managers is that if they manage badly, the resources can be transferred to new uses. This process can be summed up in the right to own and transfer property.

In order to work, however (and this is a third condition), property has to be embodied in a system of civil law which allows contracts between willing buyers and willing sellers to be enforced.

These are minimum conditions. They give protection against public power but not against private economic power. The key word is *willing* buyers and sellers; monopoly or cartels can distort such systems. This calls for a state regulatory function, which can take two forms – one positive and the other negative or at least enabling. The positive action is an active competition policy (our fourth essential feature). The negative solution, at least in a small country and in the absence of multinational firms, is to maintain open frontiers to goods, services, capital and labour from overseas. This need not be completely free trade. A government policy committed to uniform and low rates of protection against imports would provide an important bulwark against anti-competitive behaviour.

Fifth, the state clearly has a role in a market economy beyond that of night watchman as partially described above. Apart from the classic functions of providing the legal framework within which economic activity may take place, as well as structures for civil peace-keeping and external security, it can have and does have – throughout Western democracies – other roles. These include the management of the macro economy, and the regulation of market externalities – i.e. those costs and benefits which arise from economic activity but which are not included in the calculations of buyer and seller, and hence are excluded from the price. The costs of pollution are an obvious example of such externalities. Others are education and training, where there is a temptation to free-ride, and distributional objectives such as social insurance or health provision, where individuals may underprovide. The choice of how far down these routes a state goes is one that is constantly faced in democratic societies. There is no correct answer except that those who vote for it must also be able to change their minds. In other words, a degree of consensus is required on the extent of state regulation. That is a political rather than an economic judgment, but it is an important connection between democracy and the stability of market economics.

In considering the interplay of the state and the market, one must clearly take account of the *form* of state involvement. In the terms of the German social market economy theorists (notably Müller Armack), state intervention should be as far as possible 'marktconform': that is, it should be by way of transfers of cash to individuals rather than being tied to any particular use. Conversely, governments should not intervene in such a way as to change price relativities in markets for goods or factors of production by selective taxes or subsidies. This message should not need underlining in Eastern Europe.

The last major function of the state to be discussed is that of monetary issue. This is not a necessary function of the state but it is normally a state monopoly. It is important for the functioning of markets not just because of the possible impact on demand of badly set monetary policy but also because of the temptation that faces states to use their monetary monopoly to levy the so-called inflation tax on the populace. Further, when inflation is sustained at high levels, it can mask relative price movements and confuse resource allocation decisions. It is therefore important for the state to follow predictable and credible policies to maintain the value of the currency at home and abroad if it wishes to encourage market development.

To sum up, the essential conditions which need to be present if Eastern Europe is to move decisively away from Leninism and towards a market-based democratic society are these:

(1) a free pricing system;
(2) the right to own and transfer property;
(3) a system of civil law which, *inter alia*, includes a law of contract;
(4) an effective competition policy, including open frontiers to goods, services, capital and labour;
(5) state involvement largely in the form of transfers rather than by means of direct intervention in markets; and
(6) a central banking/monetary policy which gives confidence in the currency at home and abroad.

Having analysed the general problem and the general shape of likely policy objectives if a shift to market democracy is the final intention, let us now look in turn at each of the four countries – Poland, Hungary, Czechoslovakia and the GDR – under review.

Country analysis*
Just as it is important in general discussion of East European economies to keep in mind the diversity of the countries under investigation, so, when looking at individual countries, the converse applies.

In other words, the Leninist system has imposed a remarkable homogeneity on the economic experience of a disparate group of countries which before the postwar communist takeover had reached very different stages of development. The system has created two broad types of problem for all the new reformist governments. These are, on the one hand, systemic problems, which include the whole range of distortions intrinsic to central planning discussed in the first part of the chapter; and, on the other, macrostabilization problems, which touch essentially on the various consequences of excess demand created by the system.

* Statistical data for the four countries are given in the appendix to this chapter. The vexed question of measuring gross national product in these countries is also discussed there.

The following analysis is organized around this central distinction, which has two advantages. First, it allows ease of comparison; and, second, it shows up the many important differences at the micro policy level, and especially differences in the emphasis of previous attempts at reform, which will be crucial now in determining the correct policy-mix for bringing these respective economies into a homogeneous market-oriented system.

POLAND

The Poles have spent much of the past ten years instituting various economic reforms. The fact remains, however, that by mid-1989 the Polish economy was no closer to a market economy than it was at the beginning of the decade. An enormous debt problem, with accompanying shortages of foreign exchange, slow growth, accelerating inflation and shortages of basic goods all pointed to an economy heading for total collapse. That was the situation inherited by the Solidarity government.

The statistics and forecasts at the end of 1989 are summarized in the Appendix Table 3.2. The seriousness of the macroeconomic situation emerges clearly. This required a standard – if draconian – domestic deflation, accompanied by a shift of resources from domestic to hard-currency markets.

Systemic problems

The economic history of communist Poland is almost a textbook illustration of the general analysis set out at the beginning of the chapter. Industrial competitiveness and productivity could not be achieved within the framework of arbitrary resource allocation, which in turn depressed investment performance and managerial incentive. The pricing system in particular placed no financial discipline on enterprises. An attempt was made to correct this in 1987 with the introduction of the 'hard zloty policy', which was aimed at upgrading the role of financial variables so as to influence economic conduct. But the reform had little impact against the greatest systemic obstacle of all, excessively large enterprises (*de facto* monopolies), whose performance on pricing and output was not subject to any competitive pressures. There has, however, been some growth in the private sector, especially in agriculture, where it now accounts for two-thirds of employment, compared with 10% in the non-agricultural sector. The attempt to blend an element of contract pricing with the old administrative pricing system is a typical example of the failure of piecemeal reforms within the system.

Macrostabilization problems

Until the end of 1989 monetary policy was expansionary, with the banking system financing subsidies to consumers and to industry. The initial measures taken by the new Solidarity coalition government give further strong evidence of the depth of the systemic weaknesses in the economy. It is ironical, for instance, that the deregulation of food prices in August 1989 produced a reduction in subsidies at the expense of accelerating wages and price inflation. Despite government resolve, wages rose faster than prices, thereby dragging up inflation to absorb the excess purchasing power.

At the same time the size of the budget deficit was underestimated because of the omission of the subsidies required to finance low interest rates on bank loans. A serious attempt to tackle the problem of negative real interest rates was made in the context of the price-incomes adjustment of 1988. Nominal rates were raised sufficiently high for banking authorities to talk for the first time of 'realistic' levels. This increase was quickly overtaken, however, by rapidly mounting inflation, and during 1989 real interest rates were increasingly negative. A significant reduction of the budget deficit will depend on the successful removal of subsidies; but this has still to bear fruit. Meanwhile tax receipts have declined and enterprises are unable to make payments because of the rise in domestic wage costs. Moreover, the limited scope for domestic government borrowing owing to negative real interest rates has made the authorities heavily reliant on printing money. Thus, the root of the hyperinflation (inflation rates in December 1989 of 700–1000%) lies in the contradictions of the economic system and the consequent inability of the government to exert monetary control.

A high rate of inflation typically provokes a movement away from the use of the local currency. So, in Poland, dollar holdings represent about 70–80% of the monetary base, and this process of dollarization has the disadvantage of increasing the amount of seigniorage (the right to print money) paid to the United States. In addition, the loss of independent control of the currency results in some welfare loss. On the other hand, use of the dollar appears to provide a useful discipline for the monetary authorities.

A further problem is the way in which hyperinflation distorts trade patterns and undermines any attempt to use the exchange rate as a tool for increasing trade surpluses in order to service the external debt. Poland has a good record in hard-currency trade, but economic liberalization is likely to produce a surge in imports, and exports may not be able to increase correspondingly in view of the pressure of domestic demand and the need to adjust production to demand and competition in world markets.

On 1 January 1990 a unified exchange rate was introduced; it is essentially of the floating type, but progress towards full convertibility may not be easy to achieve. Poland has practically no official reserves and a heavy debt burden. It has not serviced its debt in full since 1981. Only 20% is owed to Western banks, with the rest being owed to Western governments. After years of difficult debt negotiations, there is now an easing of the atmosphere. The Paris Club rescheduled the Polish debt on 16 February 1990, on exceptional terms which included the postponement of all interest payments for the remainder of 1990 and repayment over 14 years. In late December 1989, the new government signed a Letter of Intent for a Stand-By Agreement (SBA) with the IMF. The programme came into effect on 1 January 1990, and was approved by the IMF Board on 12 February.

HUNGARY

Although economic reform in Hungary officially began in the 1960s, its objective was to demonstrate how market socialism, by ensuring full employment, was superior to market capitalism's mistreatment of workers in the name of efficiency. So for years a mixed system obtained, where on the one hand full employment was the priority at the cost of efficiency and labour productivity, and, on the other, decentralizing reforms were introduced promptly enough to put Hungary far ahead of the other East European countries. The right of individuals to engage in private activities and the role of entrepreneurship are recognized. But despite all these changes Hungary is still far from being a market economy.

Systemic problems
The labour market has been governed not by the aim of efficiency or

profitability but by the top priority of full employment – an emphasis that has the effect of reinforcing the high concentration of state and cooperative enterprises (full employment being assured by ensuring the survival of the employing institutions) and reducing the incentive to use labour productively. For this reason, the allocation of labour resources is completely distorted: demographic trends show a declining workforce, and despite a high participation rate (about 78%) there is apparently little surplus labour that can be transferred to the dynamic sectors. In fact, surplus labour does exist, but it is found in the overmanned state and cooperative enterprises, where the government has been reluctant to create large-scale unemployment.

Under Kadar, the Hungarian economy was hampered by a 'dual dependency': that is, managers were subject to some market disciplines while at the same time being under continuing political and social constraints. This situation was further complicated by the unreliability of such market signals as were available, given the distortions in prices, interest rates and exchange rates.

Macrostabilization problems

Kornai (1982) came to the conclusion that the 'main characteristic features of such a system – chronic shortages, strong expansion drive, quantity drive, unrestrainable investment spirit – can be observed when the price level is stable. But they would also persist if the price level began to change and a slow accelerating inflation evolved.' Indeed, in Hungary, officially 70–75% of prices have been liberalized; but, given the high concentration of Hungarian industry, this may still not lead to competitive market-pricing. Inflation is linked to the 'full employment' priority. If a firm is not in a position to meet its debt service, then the state makes additional money available to provide support. The effect of such direct state intervention is to blunt managers' incentives to improve efficiency, so these policies discourage innovation and increase inflationary pressures.

Inflation is accompanied by increasing shortages and black markets. Enterprises hide price increases behind 'quality improvements'; government statistics show only official prices, disregarding the fact that many goods are not available at the official price, but only at a higher price in certain shops or on the black market. Inflationary pressures proceed from the demand side of the economy: if there is no capital market, households are not able to use their excess of purchasing power for investment in innovative enterprises. Savings represent a delayed demand for consumer goods. The authorities have addressed the problem of excess demand by permitting open inflation while keeping wages under control.

According to Hillman (1990), inflation rates for the fiscal years 1985–9, expressed via the official consumer price index, have been, respectively, 5.3%, 8.6%, 15.7% and 17%. One element which accounts for the jump between 1987 and 1988 is the tax reform and subsidy reductions. The tax reform of 1988 introduced a value added tax and simplified taxation of enterprises as well as developing an income tax. It aimed to reduce the state's manipulation of some 60% of national income through turnover taxes on enterprises and numerous subsidies. Previously the tax system was primarily a mechanism for reallocating revenues to enterprises in accordance with their needs and not a way to redistribute income.

Hungary is encountering both domestic and international problems. The attendant changes in real wages, further acceleration of inflation and the appearance of unemployment could pose serious threats to social stability. All necessary economic policy measures that have been adopted are likely to worsen social tension. At the international level, too, Hungary faces a difficult situation. External debt service is running at $1.5 billion, and if it were not for an IMF programme, as well as the support from other sources that follows, Hungary would be unable to meet its obligations.

CZECHOSLOVAKIA

Despite numerous attempts to transform the economy (1958, 1966, 1980, 1987), Czechoslovakia remains fundamentally a command economy. The recognition in the 1980s of a declining growth rate and of industrial obsolescence led to the adoption of an 'intensive' path of development but not to a reform that could make the transition to a market economy. So this failed, too, and despite a strong rise in capital outlays, technological innovation remained slow and the industrial structure and machinery grew more outdated.

Systemic problems

Although, legally, enterprises are independent and therefore autonomous, their behaviour does not respond to market signals, being still tightly constrained both directly by the targets of output that the plan sets, and indirectly by the amount of resources at their disposal. This is typical behaviour of a 'reformed' command economy, where some recognition is given to the market but where management methods disregard economics. According to the OECD, the proportion of firms not meeting the requirements of the plan has risen continuously. Moreover, the 47 firms that have been trying out the new management methods since January 1988, which account for some 19% of the country's industrial output, have all performed poorly – evidence of their dependence on an economic environment still ruled by the old methods.

Given the state of mismanagement and waste of resources in the employing structures, it is not surprising that the labour force, too, is badly allocated. Some sectors are overmanned, while others – notably services – have considerable shortages. Labour mobility as in other centrally planned economies is low, constrained by a housing shortage and a policy of discriminatory rent subsidies.

The reform of wholesale prices in January 1989 set the new prices according to the 'cost plus' principle, whereby volume of output is replaced by profit as the performance indicator. 'Profit', however, turned out to be yet another way for the planning authorities to control the behaviour of the firm. The amount of profit to which particular enterprises are entitled depends on the amount of capital stock and level of manufacturing costs. For example, if profit increases as a result of cost reduction, it will be punitively taxed, the increase being judged unjustifiable. This shows that the emphasis remains on income distribution rather than on efficiency.

Since 1982, some steps have been taken towards contract pricing of consumer goods (non-basic goods). Although an extension of this price mechanism is envisaged for wholesale prices, it is not satisfactory because the domestic pricing system remains an instrument of control over enterprises. It has no role in giving signals to influence economic decision-making. Another clear example of a fundamental economic feature of centrally planned economies: absolute prices do not equilibrate supply and demand for any product, and relative prices do not reflect opportunity costs.

Macrostabilization problems
Excess demand is much better controlled than in the other East

European economies; both open and hidden inflation remain low. Yet, according to Rychetnik (1989, p. 9), there is a potential monetary overhang, and an important proportion of it is represented by 'forced' savings due to shortages and to the distorted consumption pattern (e.g. basic foodstuffs are subsidized).

Until the reform of the banking system in January 1990, money was related only passively to the physical side of economic activity: i.e. the flows of materials, energy, and semi-finished and finished products. Under the new regulations, the state bank became the central bank and three commercial banks have been created. All the tools for monetary policy (if a money market develops further) and credit for entrepreneurial activity now seem in place.

External trade is very important to Czechoslovakia for the rehabilitation of its antiquated productive structures. Since 1984, when, according to the OECD (1989), it had a substantial trade surplus with non-socialist countries of about $800 million, the country's trade deficit has rapidly widened (with a notable increase in imports of machinery and equipment). This has led to an increase in the developed countries' share of Czechoslovakia's non-socialist imports at the expense of the less developed countries. The deterioration of Czechoslovakia's trade balance was followed by a steady rise in debt; but, despite over-aggregation of official data, it is likely that its debt-service obligations will remain manageable.

Thanks to its low debt burden, Czechoslovakia can attract some of the best terms in the international market. This advantage can be used to increase imports which could contribute to the modernization of its obsolete production system and to enhance competitiveness in the external market.

The achievement of full convertibility for the Czechoslovak crown, or koruna, will depend on two conditions being met. First, the exchange rate will have to be unified. Some progress was made in January 1989, when the exchange-rate structure was simplified by the creation of a single commercial rate, a reduction in tourist rates, and a cross-rate system which enhances the value of hard-currency trade relative to trade within the CMEA group. The second condition concerns the more fundamental matter of the market-oriented reform of the domestic economy. This is well illustrated by the nominal devaluation in May 1989 of the currency's commercial exchange rate, which in reality was meaningless without any reform of the complex structure of subsidized production and pricing; and, of course, the previous authorities had not the slightest intention of removing this essential feature of the centrally planned system.

In order to make convertibility a worthwhile policy objective, therefore, an effective system of price formation must be set in place, thus linking domestic prices to world market forces. A first step in this direction was taken by the new government in January 1990, when the koruna was sharply devalued.

GDR

East Germany is still an unreformed command economy. As with the other early reforms in the region, the 1963 reform was a way of trying to make the socialist regime more efficient and powerful. It was designed as an interrelated system of economic levers (e.g. prices, taxes and interest rates) to achieve state goals more efficiently by combining centralism and the autonomy of economic units. For example, some combines (groups of enterprises) were set on a market-based footing· of cost-accounting and profitability, while having greater flexibility to engage in foreign trade. Some of the combines competed effectively with the West.

The GDR consistently had one of the higher reported growth rates in the area (but the 1989 rate of only 2% was the lowest for decades after the exodus of workers to the West). It therefore insisted that no comprehensive reform was needed because small adjustments in the system of economic management were made as they became necessary. But severe structural problems facing the East German economy (such as the exodus of workers, the collapse of the free exchange rate and the surge of GDR shoppers to the West) will force a market system.

Systemic problems
The combine was designed as a way of reinforcing centralization in a rather dialectic way: decentralization to small units in order to delegate command while leaving the 'centre' to concentrate on 'strategic' matters. The enterprises merged into combines are legally and economically independent units; but state plan-targets are delegated to them and they operate on the basis of economic accountancy. This leads to a mixture of political and economic management in which, as in the other East European countries, the

political always prevails. In agriculture, too, cooperative ownership accounts for about 87% of the land. But individual agriculture as well as industrial production was encouraged in the GDR earlier than in other East European countries.

Labour is a scarce factor of production in manufacturing as well as in agriculture (reinforced by the exodus of 344,000 workers, the majority of whom were skilled); and the trainee situation is precarious, increasing the need for foreign workers. It is no less true that the labour force is badly managed in order to justify the 'full employment' principle. Thus everything from the natural cycle of the labour supply to a decision not to fill vacant posts is ascribed to socialist rationalization. According to the Deutsches Institut für Wirtschaftsforschung, over 90% of the workers 'saved' remain in their enterprises, which keeps structural changes across sectors to a minimum.

There have been some changes in the pricing system but no radical reform. The increase in industrial prices carried out in the period 1976–86 and the agricultural price reform of 1984–6 did not lead to competitive market pricing. They were all part of the 'levers'. The agricultural price reform was designed to adapt the economic conditions of agriculture to those of industry and, as in the industrial sector, to stimulate individual production within very strict limits. This was considered necessary for the system to work more efficiently and to serve the socialist market better. Thus, in a classic socialist way, the basic primary goods are heavily subsidized while the so-called 'luxury goods' (e.g. cars) are heavily taxed.

Macrostabilization problems
The GDR has apparently controlled the growth of excess demand, and measured inflation remains comparatively low. The characteristic of East Germany, however, was concealed inflation. This is reflected in an increasing overhang of excess purchasing power and a scarcity of the goods, which are included in the official price index and for which prices are maintained at a stable level. As the OECD (1989) notes, even with the tacit acceptance of concealed inflation, subsidies to maintain stable prices now claim a very large part of the budget. But, with the opening of the monetary border, free monetary flows from West Germany will absorb the monetary overhang (an estimated 150 billion marks are held in East German savings

accounts). This, combined with the removal of price subsidies, may trigger high domestic inflation. Another result could be massive capital flight to West Germany, further weakening the currency and strengthening the purchasing power of foreigners (a far more significant factor than the much feared 500 million marks now held outside the country). This shows the strong need for currency reform (the Ostmark is still technically inconvertible, but black-market trading drove the exchange rate down to around 6:1 against the DM in early 1990); but the priority is economic reform. Another difficulty is the unreliability of economic statistics, which is a consequence of the system.

The task for East Germany is complicated by its privileged position vis-à-vis the FRG, which is draining away its labour and destroying its currency. The issues arising from a possible unification of the two countries' currencies are discussed in the next chapter.

To conclude, despite the exodus of labour and its currency problem, the GDR is better placed than other East European countries to carry through reforms because it has the highest growth rates in the region, a skilled workforce, a private sector of small firms, and a moderate debt burden.

References

Deutsches Institut für Wirtschaftsforschung (1989). *The GDR Economy in the First Half of 1989*, pp. 4–8, November.

Economic Commission for Europe [ECE] (1989). *Economic Bulletin for Europe*, vol. 41, November.

Hillman, A.L. (1990). 'Macroeconomic Policy in Hungary and its Microeconomic Implications', *European Economy*, May.

Kornai, J. (1982). *Growth, Shortage and Efficiency: A Macrodynamic Model of the Socialist Economy*, Oxford, Oxford University Press.

Mises, L. von (1972). 'Economic Calculation in the Socialist Commonwealth', in A. Nove and D.M. Nuti, eds., *Socialist Economics*, Harmondsworth, Middlesex, Penguin.

OECD (1989). 'East-West Trade and Financial Relations Developments in 1987–88 and Future Prospects', in *Financial Market Trends*, February.

Valenta, F. (1989). 'Framework of Economic Reform in Czechoslovakia', Economic Commission for Europe, *Economic Studies*, no. 1, pp. 20–27.

Statistical Appendix

The following tables present estimates for some important economic indicators for the countries of Eastern Europe under review. Economic data for these countries are unfortunately of a poor quality. Because of their membership in the IMF, the economic data available for Hungary and Poland are more reliable than those for Czechoslovakia and the GDR, but are still not very satisfactory.

There is a fundamental difficulty in determining GNP in dollar terms. Broadly speaking there are two approaches: either to use the official exchange rate or to deduce a rate based on purchasing power parities (PPPs). These methods give unrealistically low and high figures respectively (the range is indicated in the tables). The first method could be applied, in the case of Hungary and Poland, to the International Financial Statistics (IFS) tables of the IMF for the data in domestic currencies, but official exchange rates, since they are fixed arbitrarily, do not provide a sound basis for converting domestic currency figures into dollars. In any case, not all of the countries calculate GNP, preferring to refer to Net Material Product (NMP), which is equal to net domestic product less the net value added to the non-material service sector. Very often, too, the East European economies publish only growth rates without giving the NMP figure itself. The second method, which has been used by the CIA, is based on the UN's International Comparison Project (ICP) and is capable of producing only approximate results (see CIA, *Handbook*).

Little weight can be attached to official growth figures, since, generally, they do no more than reflect the unreality of official pricing policy and therefore ignore underlying inflation. Whereas inflation figures for Poland and Hungary are in the right range, those for Czechoslovakia and the GDR are quite unrealistic, which suggests that growth in these countries may have been overestimated.

The balance-of-payments figures are based on IMF sources. The entries for external debt and reserves draw on OECD and BIS sources, which point out the probable omission of some debt owed to non-reporting banks, particularly those in the CMEA.

Soft-currency trade figures have been calculated by the IMF for Poland and Hungary by converting transferable roubles to dollars at official exchange rates. As the exchange rate is arbitrary, the estimates of soft-currency trade are useful only in giving a very general idea of magnitude, and there is no basis for comparing them with the hard-currency figures.

Table 3.2 Poland

	1986	1987	1988	1989 (est.)
Population (m)	37.6	37.8	37.8	
GDP ($ bn)[a]			165 (52–276)	
of which:[b]				
Industry (%)			33	
Agriculture (%)			24	
Oth. prod. sectors (%)			24	
Non-prod. sectors (%)			19	
GDP per head ($)[a]			4300 (1680–7270)	
GDP growth (%)[c]	4.2	2.0	4.1	−1.0
CPI inflation (% change on prev. year)[c]	18	25	74	700
Balance of payments				
Hard currency ($ bn)[c]				
Current account	−0.7	−0.4	−0.6	−2.0
Exports	5.3	6.2	7.2	7.5
of which:[b]				
Mach. & equip. (%)	28	24	23	22
Fuels (%)	18	15	12	12
Non-food raw mat. (%)	26	29	34	35
Food (%)	17	18	17	17
Ind. cons. goods (%)	11	14	14	14
Imports	−4.3	−5.1	−6.3	−7.5
of which:[b]				
Mach. & equip. (%)	30	29	27	28
Fuels (%)	5	4	5	6
Non-food raw mat. (%)	40	43	42	37
Food (%)	14	13	14	17
Ind. cons. goods (%)	11	11	12	12
External debt[d]	33.5	38.8	39.1	42.0
Deposits at BIS banks				
Official reserves	0.7	1.5	2.1	1.7
Debt service	6.2	6.3	6.8	
Debt service ratio (%)	63	79	76	89
Soft currency[c]				
Exports	6.2	5.7	6.0	6.0
Imports	6.6	5.7	5.8	5.4

[a]Central estimate based on 1985 PPPs. Lower figure of range is calculated at official exchange rate; higher is from CIA handbook.
[b]Source: Planecom.
[c]Source: IMF.
[d]Source: *The International Financial Situation of East European Countries* (OECD, 1990).

Table 3.3 Hungary

	1986	1987	1988	1989 (est.)
Population (m)			10.6	
GDP ($ bn)[a]			61 (19.92)	
of which:[b]				
Industry (%)			32	
Agriculture (%)			24	
Oth. prod. sectors (%)			24	
Non-prod. sectors (%)			20	
GDP per head ($)[a]			5780 (1800–8660)	
GDP growth (%)	0.7[c]	3.9[c]	1.1[d]	
CPI inflation (% change on				
prev. year)[c]	5.3	8.7	15.7	20.0
Balance of payments				
Hard currency ($ bn)[c]				
Current account	−1.4	−0.8	−0.6	−1.4
Exports	4.1	5.1	5.8	6.3
of which:[b]				
Mach. & equip. (%)	17	16	16	15
Fuels (%)	6	6	4	3
Non-food raw mat. (%)	35	36	38	41
Food (%)	26	25	26	27
Ind. cons. goods (%)	16	17	16	14
Imports	−4.7	−4.9	−5.1	−5.4
of which:[b]				
Mach. & equip. (%)	25	27	28	30
Fuels (%)	7	6	3	1
Non-food raw mat. (%)	44	44	48	47
Food (%)	12	11	11	12
Ind. cons. goods (%)	12	12	10	10
External debt[c]	15.1	17.7	17.3	20.0
Deposits at BIS banks				
Official reserves[f]	3.8	2.8	2.4	
Debt service	3.7	3.4	3.4	
Debt service ratio (%)[c]	65	50	54	41
Soft currency[c]				
Exports	5.0	4.7	4.5	
Imports	5.0	5.0	4.4	

[a]Central estimate based on 1985 PPPs. Lower figure of range is calculated at official exchange rate; higher is from CIA handbook.
[b]Source: Planecom.
[c]Source: IMF.
[d]Source: CIA handbook.
[e]Source: *The International Financial Situation of East European Countries* (OECD, 1990).
[f]Calculated residually as IFS-reported total trade less hard currency trade.

Table 3.4 Czechoslovakia

	1986	1987	1988	1989 (est.)
Population (m)			15.6	15.7[c]
GDP ($ bn)[a]			115 (115–158)	
of which:[b]				
Industry (%)			40	
Agriculture (%)			16	
Oth. prod. sectors (%)			25	
Non-prod. sectors (%)			19	
GDP per head ($)[a]			7340 (7340–10140)	
GDP growth (%)	2.1	1.0	1.4	
CPI inflation (% change on prev. year)	0	1	1	
Balance of payments				
Hard currency ($ bn)				
Current account	0.4	0.1	0.1	
Exports	4.2	4.5	4.9	5.4
of which:[b]				
Mach. & equip. (%)	31	27	24	24
Fuels (%)	8	9	8	9
Non-food raw mat. (%)	34	36	40	40
Food (%)	8	8	8	8
Ind. cons. goods (%)	19	20	20	19
Imports	4.0	4.7	5.1	5.6
of which:[b]				
Mach. & equip. (%)	36	40	41	43
Fuels (%)	2	3	2	3
Non-food raw mat. (%)	43	40	39	38
Food (%)	12	10	11	9
Ind. cons. goods (%)	7	7	7	7
External debt[e]	4.3	5.3	5.7	6.2
Deposits at BIS banks	1.2	1.6	1.7	1.9
Debt service	0.8	0.9	0.9	
Debt service ratio (%)[e]	17	18	16	18
Soft currency[f]				
Exports	8.7	8.2	8.2	
Imports	9.1	8.2	6.6	

[a]Central estimate based on 1985 PPPs. Lower figure of range is calculated at official exchange rate; higher is from CIA handbook.
[b]Source: Planecom.
[c]*World Population Prospects, 1988* (UN Publications, sales no. E88 xiii.7).
[d]Source: CIA handbook.
[e]Source: *The International Financial Situation of East European Countries* (OECD, 1990).
[f]Converted at the official exchange rate.

Table 3.5 GDR

	1986	1987	1988	1989 (est.)
Population (m)			16.6	
GDP ($ bn)[a]			145 (88–209)	
of which:[b]				
Industry (%)			45	
Agriculture (%)			12	
Oth. prod. sectors (%)			24	
Non-prod. sectors (%)			19	
GDP per head ($)[a]			8745 (5320–12608)	
GDP growth (%)[c]	1.5	1.8	1.8	
CPI inflation (% change on prev. year)	2	1	1	
Balance of payments				
Hard currency ($ bn)[d]				
Current account	0.9	1.1	0.7	0.5
Exports	8.9	8.9	9.1	9.8
of which:[b]				
Mach. & equip. (%)	16	17	17	17
Fuels (%)	9	9	7	7
Non-food raw mat. (%)	41	40	43	43
Food (%)	10	8	8	9
Ind. cons. goods (%)	24	26	25	24
Imports	8.5	8.6	9.1	9.8
of which:[b]				
Mach. & equip. (%)	21	28	30	31
Fuels (%)	7	7	5	6
Non-food raw mat. (%)	56	49	49	47
Food (%)	5	5	5	5
Ind. cons. goods (%)	11	11	11	11
External debt[e]	15.7	18.9	19.5	21.2
Deposits at BIS banks	7.5	9.0	9.9	
Debt service	3.1	3.4	4.2	
Debt service ratio (%)[e]	46	50	72	70
Soft currency[f]				
Exports	33.3	41.0	42.3	
Imports	32.2	39.6	40.6	

[a]Central estimate based on 1985 PPPs. Lower figure of range is calculated at official exchange rate; higher is from ECE Secretariat Common Data Base, derived from national or CMEA statistics.
[b]Source: Planecom.
[c]Source: CIA handbook.
[d]Includes intra-German trade and financial relations.
[e]Source: *The International Financial Situation of East European Countries* (OECD, 1990).
[f]Converted at the official exchange rate.

4

THE AGENDA FOR REFORM

J.M.C. Rollo and Brigitte Granville

Chapters 2 and 3 set out the nature of the problem facing the countries in Eastern Europe: how to move from Leninist political and economic structures to democratic and market-based systems. This task raises social and political issues, economic policy difficulties, both at the micro and at the macro level, and environmental problems. They are all interrelated, and progress on one front is often related to progress on another.

The nature of this interrelationship is most clearly demonstrated in the connection between macrostabilization problems and systemic problems. For the countries under review (Czechoslovakia perhaps excepted), an immediate macroeconomic stabilization is required. Success will depend on shifting resources quickly into the hard-currency-traded goods sector and away from domestic consumption. This in turn depends on raising prices in the traded goods sector relative to those in other sectors. To do that, the exchange rate must fall and domestic pricing systems must react. Thus convertibility of the exchange rate and freedom of prices are imperative.

Some of the impact will also have to come from deflating domestic demand directly by squeezing monetary and fiscal policy. To do the former effectively needs a capital market; to do the latter requires political support and democratic legitimacy to cope with the inevitable fall in real money incomes, bankruptcies and unemployment. The last two issues point to the need for effective capital markets, so as to allow resources to be switched quickly from old to new uses, and for social insurance, so as to maintain political support among the temporary unemployed. The pressing nature of the stabilization problem, however, does not give time to set up the background institutions required to ensure the longer-term stability of market mechanisms.

As discussed in Chapter 3, systemic change requires not merely a pricing system but also rights of property ownership and transfer, and civil commercial laws to which the state is subject, guaranteeing contracts. Subsumed in these conditions is the need to have, on the one hand, institutions which can handle the new transactions – central banks with real powers, commercial banks, bond markets – so that government can separate fiscal and monetary policy, and, on the other, stock markets to assess the performance and hence the value of firms. Competition policies must be put in place which ensure that newly emerging state monopolies do not abuse their market power.

Jeffrey Sachs, in a famous analogy, states that a chasm cannot be crossed in two bounds (*The Economist*, 13 January 1990); the difficulty in the case of Eastern Europe is that is may not be possible to cross it in *one* bound. There is no conceivable way in which all these changes can happen simultaneously. The immediate question is therefore one of ordering. And, to be fair to Sachs and others, the programme for Poland launched on 1 January 1990 is at the same time radical while paying attention to ordering and having a three-year time horizon. Before turning to specific countries, however, we need to develop some general propositions on ordering.

Macrostabilization measures
Where the balance of payments is in a deficit which cannot be sustained by long-term capital inflows and domestic inflation is rising, the first priority is to attain internal and external balance. This calls for the immediate depreciation of the currency and a deflation of domestic demand so as to increase net exports and control inflation. This, however, takes time. In the interval, essential imports have to be funded and care has to be taken to ensure that the currency is not forced down so low that, despite an apparently sufficient domestic deflation, inflation is made worse. The necessary domestic policy instruments in this case are a monetary policy which

maintains real interest rates at levels sufficient to reduce demand for credit and a fiscal policy which acts to reduce real domestic consumption in the government and personal sector. Foreign creditors can contribute by making available sufficient foreign exchange to bridge any current-account deficit and to allow the adjusting country to hold reserves sufficient to defend a realistic long-term exchange rate.

Systemic reforms

The conventional approach to removing systemic economic distortions is to start with internal distortions. Once domestic markets for goods, services and factors of production are functioning, the external distortions can be tackled; notably trade policy can be liberalized and currencies made convertible. The situation in Eastern Europe may not allow this orderly approach. To correct balance-of-payments deficits needs convertibility of the currency if depreciation is to be effective. The sheer size of the state sector and its monopolistic structure suggest that the scale of capital markets necessary to privatize will not be present for many years, and that the removal of monopoly power will be difficult. Nevertheless, a liberal trade policy would put considerable competitive pressures on large state firms, while outside capital markets could help to fund the privatization process.

The issue of the reform of CMEA trade, too, suggests that the external sector is a priority. At official exchange rates, intra-CMEA trade represents more than half of trade (itself very low) in these countries. At market exchange rates and world prices, it would no doubt be less important – at least on the export side. Because of the entirely fictitious nature of the pricing and exchange rates, such trade has had a severely deforming effect on productive structures and even on short-term monetary management in Eastern Europe. Converting this trade to a hard-currency basis should be a priority. To the extent that Eastern Europe depends on low-priced Soviet raw materials, in particular for energy, hard-currency pricing may need to be phased in or financed by bridging loans. Realistic energy pricing is important not merely for the efficiency and competitiveness of the productive sector but also for environmental reasons.

After external policy and goods markets, the next task must be the freeing up of factor markets. The capital market, in particular, should be an early target for action. In most cases – Hungary is perhaps the only exception – capital markets will have to be invented. This means taking the control of capital allocation away from central planners and putting it in the hands of private-sector institutions. That requires not just credit institutions such as banks, which can advance loans, short- and long-term, but also bond markets, necessary for separating fiscal from monetary policy, and equity markets, necessary for spreading risks more widely and in due course disposing of monopolistic state structures. The latter is an enormous undertaking. Even in Hungary some 90% of the productive sector is still in state enterprises. No domestic equity market could absorb that quickly. The role of privatization in the possible development of domestic capital markets is complicated, for it raises political as well as technical issues. Nor is it only enterprises which are to be privatized; land and housing are also in the state sector in many of these countries.

Perhaps the quickest answer to the privatization problem is simply to give the assets away. The question, then, is to whom. It might seem obvious that housing, for example, should be given to the sitting tenants. But the same may not be true of land (the owners before nationalization may be known, or it may be farmed collectively). The case of enterprises is even more complicated. Just giving them to their current workers and managers may be no more than rewarding the *nomenklatura* who were at the heart of the old system. In any case, many enterprises exist only as a result of past state support, and on grounds of fairness the benefits should go to those who funded them.

There are a number of ways in which this might be done. State equity funds might be set up to cover all industries, and shares in each fund given away in equal lumps. This raises the question of what the connection would be between the value of the shares in the equity fund and the performance of any individual enterprise, as well as the role of the shareholder.

A more realistic approach might be to issue shares in each enterprise but to give them to specially set up, fully funded state pension funds which could buy and sell them as well as buying and selling shares in any new domestic companies and overseas companies. Citizens would receive benefits in pensions, and there would be institutional shareholders with sufficient clout to discipline management.

The alternative to giving away these assets is to sell them. This could be important from a fiscal standpoint. The new governments need to stabilize fiscal policy and, as the British government found in the 1980s, a judicious programme of privatization can ease fiscal policy constraints. Lack of capital markets slows that process. Privatization can of course be used to build up domestic capital markets in conjunction with foreign capital markets. And some assets could be privatized quickly. Housing is the obvious candidate. Sitting tenants could be offered preferential prices, which would have the added benefit of absorbing some, if not all, of the monetary overhang.

The lack of domestic buyers for enterprises is likely to be a problem in the early days. This, along with the difficulty in establishing the potential and actual performance of firms, will keep the capital value of enterprises low, and hence will allow foreigners to buy up cheap. In principle this is what is necessary. These are high-risk investments, and it is only with the attraction of low purchase prices that they will receive the management and investment that will allow them to flourish. There is, however, a potential political problem, as attitudes to foreign inward investment in Western countries show. At the extreme this might prejudice the opening up of these economies.

Considerations of fairness (including the need not to reward the old *nomenklatura*), the fiscal requirements of the government and practicality all argue for selling existing state assets rather than giving them away. An open trade policy would help to ensure that monopoly powers are not exploited while the necessarily slow process of privatization goes ahead.

In practical terms, in the near future, there are two priorities: to develop small and medium-size firms in the domestic market and to attract foreign capital in takeovers, joint ventures and greenfield investments. These two priorities suggest that early attention should be paid to banking and venture capital institutions, and to regulations which provide foreign capital with long-term guarantees on inward investment. Local-practice regulations on ownership, and accountancy rules which allow performance to be assessed and assets to be transferred, will then set the scene for privatization in the long term as equity markets develop.

The labour force in these countries is both their greatest asset and the source of most immediate political danger. Freedom of pricing, reductions in subsidy and increased foreign competition will all put domestic firms under intense pressure to cut costs and raise productivity. This will inevitably lead to redundancies. At the same time, any domestic deflation will reduce the real standard of living of those at work. There is no alternative to this process. The more flexible the labour market is, the shorter the adjustment period will be. Experience in Western economies – notably Britain in the 1970s and 1980s – shows that even in relatively flexible economies adjustment can take time and unemployment can reach substantial proportions.

In order to provide the necessary political breathing-space, aid will have to be given to those worst affected. This has its own dangers. The public expenditure costs will slow the fiscal adjustment. If the aid is too high, or available for too long, it will delay adjustment in the labour market.

For the longer term, training in new skills and the updating of old skills should be the priority. Some of this will happen in any case as the private sector expands and presents fresh incentives to improve personal skills. The move of 400,000 workers into the Polish private sector shows what an important channel of change this is. Foreign firms equally have a role. The new technology they bring will require them to train their workforces.

Working abroad is potentially a major source of relief to short-term labour market problems and longer-term training. Workers who temporarily go overseas bring back skills and often capital, as well as providing foreign-exchange flows in the short term as they support their family at home.

Finally, Eastern Europe's environmental problems must be tackled. Chapter 3 argued that the main causes of the high levels of pollution in the region were, first, the way in which centralized economic structures encouraged mismanagement and waste of resources; and, second, the dependence on coal or lignite as a primary fuel for electricity generation. These factors call for two different types of response.

The first problem will respond to the introduction of market forces. As managers become more cost-conscious, they will economize on energy use, reduce commodity dependence and cut waste. As domestic structures become stronger, more attention will need to be paid to environmental policy standards, and to improving sewage treatment, for example. The lignite problem could be managed by fitting expensive gas extraction equipment. From a cost point of view, however, it would be better to change the fuel-mix towards natural gas. This would improve energy efficiency and reduce atmospheric pollutants at the same time.

Country analysis

As we saw in Chapter 3, the problems facing the East European economies can be divided into two main categories: problems of macrostabilization and systemic problems. The countries will have to tackle these issues simultaneously and sequentially – a combination of root-and-branch reform and small steps. In this, they will need a wide range of assistance from competent multilateral organizations (the World Bank and the IMF, the EEC and the OECD) as well as from individual Western countries.

We will begin by looking at the urgent stabilization policies planned and at those which, to varying degrees, are already under way. We will then consider the various legal and institutional reforms necessary for an irreversible transition to a market economy. It is a commonplace by now that nothing of the kind has ever been attempted before, and that this is quite uncharted terrain. It is the uncertainty regarding the social costs of the transition which is particularly acute. Public support for fundamental reforms may be difficult to sustain in societies which have officially been free of inequalities and unemployment. For this reason, the chances of success will depend heavily, as already noted, on the establishment of an effective system of safety nets and welfare measures.

An analysis along these lines is easier for Poland and Hungary, since they are the most advanced reformers (and the main features of their IMF programmes are already known). The policy agenda in Czechoslovakia and the GDR is much less certain (though for different reasons in each), and we can only sketch out possible scenarios which may soon be overtaken by events.

POLAND

The adjustment programme came into force on 1 January 1990. Its twin aims are to stabilize the economy as rapidly and firmly as possible, and to effect the transition to a market economy. This survey is divided into three sections. The first attempts to describe the stabilization programme by breaking it down into three main components: the use of the exchange rate and wages as instruments to defeat inflation; fiscal policy; and the introduction of a monetary and credit policy that is sufficiently tight both to contain the excess demand and prices flowing from economic liberalization and to encourage a shift from hard-currency to domestic-currency deposits. In the second section, we will consider the authorities' plans for attacking systemic problems. They have two priorities: first, the comprehensive liberalization of all prices and foreign trade and exchange in order to balance supply and demand and remove the distortions preventing efficient allocation of resources; and, second, the creation of a range of institutions which will encourage the emergence of a market economy. The third section describes the various 'safety nets' and forms of social protection necessary for the smooth implementation of such a programme.

(i)   Macrostabilization measures

The anchors

The authorities aim to realign the official zloty exchange rate with the free market rate. On 1 January the exchange rate for current transactions was unified at Zl 9500 = $1. This amounted to a real effective devaluation of 40% compared with the fourth quarter of 1989 in terms of retail prices; and, measured against wage costs, the devaluation was even deeper. The realignment of the official rate may have a knock-on effect on the free rate, and any lasting discrepancy of more than 10% between the two would undermine the effectiveness of exchange-rate policy. This devaluation will of course result in increased import prices and reduced purchasing power. Yet this need not have an inflationary effect, since it will do no more than regularize the existing use of the free exchange market and hard currency for domestic transactions. Indeed, the government plans to hold the rate stable during the first three months of the programme precisely in order to counter inflationary expectations. Thereafter, to prevent significant depletion of reserves, the real exchange rate will be kept in line with planned increases in labour costs, thereby preserving competitiveness without relaxing the brake on inflation.

The use of exchange-rate policy to protect Poland's meagre

reserves will be reinforced by external assistance. The government has taken out a $215 million bridging loan with the Bank for International Settlements (BIS) and the US Treasury, and a stabilization fund amounting to about $1 bn has been set up to provide a back-up supply of reserves, although it will be drawn down only as a last resort.

The second main weapon in the fight against inflation is wages policy. Maintaining nominal wage increases below the rate of inflation and the level of domestic demand below nominal incomes are fundamental for stabilizing the economy. The problem is a political one, since it is a matter of persuading the people to accept wage restraint. In consultation with the IMF, the government has worked out a range of fiscal instruments to enhance wage discipline. If all goes well, this policy will result in a reduction in real wages of almost a third between 1989 and 1990. It will also be important in preserving firms' viability following the loss of the effective subsidy – worth about 5% on sales – provided by negative real interest rates.

Although incomes policy is crucial in the short term, experience shows that in the longer term it is no substitute for effective fiscal and monetary policies.

Fiscal policy
Budgetary discipline depends upon reducing subsidies on production and consumption. Thus the government plans in 1990 the almost complete elimination of subsidies on food and agricultural inputs and the gradual phasing out of coal subsidies. Salaries in the state sector will be adjusted down to the levels of the non-governmental sectors. These reductions in government expenditure will be partly offset by increased transfers amounting to about 6% of GDP, notably for external debt service, new welfare schemes, including the social insurance fund, and other current expenditure. On the revenue side, almost all income tax reliefs will be abolished. The government has undertaken not to borrow, either directly or indirectly, from the central bank.

Achieving such fiscal discipline will not be easy. The policy will be vulnerable not only to pressures on spending, but also to the uncertain outlook for profits, which will affect the yield from corporate taxation.

Monetary and credit policy

The programme assigns two tasks to this policy: to halt the excessive expansion of demand by controlling the financial indiscipline of firms; and to reinstate the zloty as a store of value.

It will be no easy task to replace a system of centralized direct credit supply with a decentralized system. However, the Polish authorities have made a start. The National Bank of Poland has been given independent status and responsibility for guaranteeing domestic monetary stability. Nine local banks have been set up, and there has been a pilot privatization of one of the these. In spite of these reforms, effective control of banking liquidity will remain difficult. There is neither a money market nor a capital market, and the sole methods of saving are bank deposits and a few securities. Nor should the inexperience of firms in the sort of investment appraisal which would make interest rates an efficient means of credit rationing be forgotten. There is therefore a risk of credit explosion. With the technical assistance of the IMF and other institutions, the authorities nevertheless plan during 1990 to create money and capital markets, introduce new accountancy regulations and encourage competition between banks.

Despite the constraints to which monetary policy is subject, the authorities are determined to maintain high real interest rates to encourage saving and discourage consumption. To that end, they raised the rate of loans from the central to the commercial banks from 7% per month to 36% in January and February 1990. This is expected to be well above the rate of inflation in these two months.

(ii) Systemic reforms

According to the principles of competition and the free market, the government abolished price controls on almost all goods and services at the end of January 1990. Only about 10% of prices are still fixed by the state. (The main ones are: rents, public utility services, public transport fares, solid fuels and other areas where there are monopoly powers.)

Also in January, the government extensively liberalized exchange and trade arrangements. Foreign exchange is now freely available at the official rate to individuals and firms for most transactions. Firms are now required to surrender all foreign-exchange receipts to the monetary authorities. All quantitative restrictions on imports from the hard-currency area have been lifted, and a unified customs tariff for commercial and consumer goods has been introduced, with temporary surcharges for certain consumer goods. In addition, the number of export commodities subject to quota has been halved and the regulations governing participation in foreign trade have been greatly simplified.

In the legal and institutional sphere, the government plans to introduce over the next few years a whole range of new laws and institutions, which fall into five main categories:

(1) Privatization of a large number of firms, for which the necessary legislation will be completed during 1990. The process will be divided into stages and spread over a number of years, with a few pilot schemes in 1990. It will be based on public offers of sale open to all, including foreign investors.

(2) The establishment of a stock exchange and a capital market.

(3) A reform of the bankruptcy laws, with a view to encouraging financial discipline in firms by enabling creditors to initiate bankruptcy proceedings when necessary.

(4) The introduction of new anti-monopoly laws in order to encourage competition; surviving restrictions on the creation of new firms will be abolished.

(5) The modernization of the banking system, with the technical assistance of the IMF and the World Bank.

This year, and again with the help of the IMF, the government plans to prepare the ground for a thorough reform of the mechanisms governing trade between members of the CMEA. Its aim is to limit the scope of their trade, which acts as a brake on the transformation of the economy by allowing firms to be dependent on the undemanding Soviet market, thus isolating them from world competition.

(iii) Social safety nets

Such a radical transformation must inevitably involve high social costs – at least in the short term. It will be important, therefore, that the government make sufficient provision for welfare benefits without distorting the necessary incentive structure. The government's new social protection plan has three main features:

(1) an action plan to provide benefits in cash and in kind for the most disadvantaged;

73

(2) family and old-age pension allowances, which will be reassessed on a quarterly basis; and
(3) a Labour Fund to support the newly unemployed, financed by a special tax on firms' payrolls as well as from ordinary government revenue.

Sufficient funds have been budgeted in 1990 for 400,000 beneficiaries; but there are fears that unemployment could reach a million or more (*The Financial Times*, 7 January 1990).

HUNGARY

Hungary experienced low growth rates throughout the 1980s, and this resulted in an increase in the debt burden relative to GNP. The two problems are interlinked. Accelerated growth would lighten the debt burden; on the other hand, debt is a constraint on growth, so substantial relief, either temporary or permanent, would permit higher growth rates. The reform programme put into effect in the Seventh Five-Year Plan (1986–90) should be seen in this perspective.

The survey is again divided into three sections. The first section will consider the macrostabilization measures (monetary, fiscal and exchange-rate policies) designed to reduce the trade deficit. The second examines the systemic measures introduced by the government to improve the working of the economy and so stimulate growth. The problems in fact have more to do with resource allocation than with macroeconomics proper, especially the apparent lack of surplus labour available for reallocation to the dynamic sectors. This labour shortage is due to unbalanced and rigid allocation, with different sectors over- and undermanned. Yet in a period of political change, the government is unwilling to risk putting thousands out of work, even temporarily. Finally, the third section briefly describes the 'safety nets' designed to ensure social cohesion.

(i) Macrostabilization measures

The anchors
In order to reduce the external current-account deficit in convertible currencies, the non-CMEA exchange rate (pegged to a basket of ten

convertible currencies*) has been periodically devalued since 1987. But, as is shown by the last devaluations of 5% and 6% in March and April 1989, this policy is not always successful. The persistent strengthening of the US dollar, which has a significant weight in the basket, and the rise in domestic inflation have together neutralized the effect of these official devaluations on the effective real exchange rate. The CMEA exchange rate is adjusted from time to time. In 1989 it was increased by 5.5% relative to the transferable rouble, in order to limit the growing balance-of-payments surplus on this trade. It is important that the scheduled introduction in 1991 of hard-currency payments between CMEA partners goes to plan. If it does, numerous obstacles caused by the current opportunities for all sorts of underhand manipulation will disappear.

It is certainly desirable at this point to have set in place a unified and convertible exchange-rate regime. But once a unified exchange rate has been established, the problem of setting it correctly and maintaining necessary flexibility will remain.

Wage controls have been a principal means of controlling private consumption. About three-quarters of the working population have been subject to direct wage control, with the rest tied to the average wage in different firms. Firms incur strong penalties (up to 1000% surtax) for awarding wage rises and profit-sharing bonuses above the authorized limits. These measures have nevertheless been combined with a system of enhanced incentives for successful firms, which allow them greater freedom in setting workers' and managers' pay. The criteria for 'success', permitting entry to this 'wage club', are limited price increases, the ability to operate without subsidies, meeting obligations to creditors, and hard-currency export earnings.

Fiscal policy
The failure of Hungary to meet agreed fiscal targets caused the breakdown of the last Stand-By Agreement with the IMF at the end of June 1989. According to Szalkai (1990), the consolidated public-sector deficit exceeded the Fund target of 4.2 bn forints by Ft 22 bn. Ironically, the reason for this deficit can be found in the distortions created by reforms in the tax system while maintaining the soft

---

* They are the Austrian schilling, the German mark, the French franc, the Italian lira, the Netherlands guilder, the pound sterling, the Swedish kroner, the Swiss franc, the US dollar and the Japanese yen.

budget constraints (as discussed in Chapter 3). Thus, while tax receipts have fallen, subsidies to loss-making firms remain.

Monetary and credit policy
Whereas the main instrument of monetary control was previously direct credit-rationing, the banking reform of 1987–8 introduced more instruments of indirect control, and the National Bank of Hungary made considerable efforts to restrict liquidity. First, commercial-bank refinancing quotas were reduced, and the compulsory reserve ratio was increased by 3%; and, second, interest rates were raised and made more flexible. Despite these measures, the present level of interest rates does not give sufficient encouragement to saving so as to discourage consumption.

(ii) Systemic reforms

Price liberalization
All prices are due to be liberalized during 1990. But, as noted in Newberry (1990), it is doubtful whether this will succeed in establishing price competition, given the monopolistic structure of Hungarian industry. This reform can succeed only if barriers to market entry are removed, or if there is sufficient potential foreign competition to impose a certain discipline on firms. Failing that, firms would not be constrained by market forces in determining prices and salaries, and would still have to be subjected to price controls. The new competition law planned for 1990, which would create a competition office empowered to control abuses, is therefore of great importance, as is the possibility of opening up the economy to further foreign competition.

Relaxation of exchange controls
Exchange controls were relaxed in January 1989 with the abolition of licences and quotas on the movement of capital or production goods, at least 40% of which derive from non-rouble imports. Other liberalization measures will be taken in stages. Imports of consumer goods remain subject to a global hard-currency quota. The liberalization of the current account began in January 1988, when restrictions on foreign travel were lifted. This led in April 1989 to an increase (from 20% to 45%) in customs duties on imported personal

goods, and a reduction in the personal duty-free allowance. Capital-account transactions have been liberalized by the removal of restrictions on participation in direct investment abroad. According to Szalkai (1990), however, these measures have contributed to the deterioration in the hard-currency balance of payments. This is a result mainly of excess domestic demand, fuelled by erratic fiscal policy, and the large current-account surplus in non-convertible currencies. Strengthened corporate revenue and liquidity have contributed to a substantial real increase in household incomes, while the opportunity to travel, combined with the relaxation of customs and exchange controls, has inevitably resulted in heavy spending on foreign travel. The measures concerning residents' accounts encouraged currency substitution and capital flight. In the circumstances, as Newberry (1990) points out, it is hardly surprising that the Hungarians are approaching import liberalization with caution.

(iii) Social safety nets

In the course of implementing market-oriented economic reforms, and now also political reforms, Hungary will need to ensure a high degree of social cohesion. This will require a range of state aids in the face of mounting inequalities and unemployment. Measures of this kind have been introduced since 1983, including temporary financial support and training grants; a national network of employment exchanges was also established. In 1987 an Employment Fund, financed from the general budget, was created to promote job creation and retraining of the unemployed; and in 1989 this fund was used to finance an unemployment benefit. It is planned in 1990 to provide this benefit from a new system of unemployment insurance, which consist of contributions from both employers and employees.

CZECHOSLOVAKIA

The Czechoslovak economy starts the process of economic reform in relatively good shape. There is no pressing external problem, hard-currency debt is low and credits outstanding from the rest of the CMEA make net debt lower still (see Chapter 3, Appendix Table 3.4). The hard-currency current account of the balance of payments is not in serious deficit. Domestically, inflation is low, fiscal policy prudent and there are as yet no shortages of food or other basic goods. Against this background, it is understandable that the initial statements of the economic team which came to power in December 1989 have been cautious about the speed and ordering of reform, if not about the degree of change necessary. The government's long-term objective is 'a market economy pure and simple' (Vaclav Claus, Finance Minister, quoted by Rodney Lord in *The Times* of 5 February 1990), and the immediate objectives are macroeconomic rather than systemic.

(i) Macroeconomic consolidation

As noted above, the issue is not so much stabilization, as in Poland, Hungary and the GDR, as consolidation. The first move by the government was to devalue the koruna by 50% on 12 January 1990. The official commercial rate, however, is still only about half the black-market rate, or indeed the tourist rate, which suggests that there is a considerable way to go on confronting the Czechoslovak traded-goods sector, and consumers generally, with prices on the world market. At the same time the process of cutting subsidies, with a view to bringing the budget into surplus, has begun. This no doubt reflects a wish to shift the pricing structure towards a market basis. But the lack of a bond market, and hence the almost immediate monetization of any fiscal deficit, indicates that the desire for fiscal surplus is part of the process of tightening monetary policy following the devaluation.

This is a sound beginning, but timidity over the level of the exchange rate, and the maintenance of different exchange rates for different sectors as a means of holding back inflation, suggest too much caution. The black market exists; at the margin choices are being made according to the market exchange rate. Thus prices will in due course start to reflect the real situation. Without a devaluation of the commercial rate to the market level, it is possible that monetary and fiscal policy will be wrongly set and enterprise decisions will be based on the wrong prices and necessary structural charges delayed.

(ii) Systemic reforms

Once more the objectives of reform are clear but the timetable is cautious. The Czechoslovaks wish to make the currency convertible, abolish trade monopolies, increase domestic competition, build up capital markets, privatize the large state enterprises. But none of these things are to happen immediately. In part this may reflect a perceived need to face the electorate with these choices and ask for approval in the May 1990 elections. Once the programme has been approved, progress may be swifter, not least because internal opposition will have been silenced (note, for example, the attitude of Trade Minister Barcak to the removal of trade monopolies, as reported by A.H. Hermann in *The Financial Times* of 25 January 1990). But early in 1990 the hesitations appear more evident than the objectives.

The outline approach seems to be a gradual alignment of the official with the market rate of exchange and a move to convertibility of the currency over an unspecified period (ten years was suggested in a profile of Deputy Prime Minister Komarek in the *Christian Science Monitor Weekly* of 12–18 January 1990). At the same time trade monopolies will be dismantled, and a new, unspecified but presumably GATT-consistent trade regime will be put in their place. In parallel with these moves to increase foreign competition, the diversification of the productive structure will begin. There seems to be no wish to rush into privatization. Rather, existing state industries will attempt to improve their efficiency through joint ventures with Western firms and in response to competitive pressures. Cooperatives, limited companies and companies in individual ownership will be encouraged. The reluctance to rush into privatization appears to reflect the lack of a capital market rather than any admiration for existing state enterprises. The emphasis on cooperatives and small firms probably reflects the view that there should be a shift away from heavy industry towards light industry and services (see Komarek as reported in the same *Christian Science Monitor* profile).

The legal bases for these changes are in preparation. A law on foreign investment, currently before the National Assembly, is likely to be in force by April 1990. This will allow foreign firms ownership rights, the right to hire and fire, the right to remit profits and the right to form joint ventures with Czech firms. There are also laws in draft which aim to remove barriers to private business (including a legally binding right to private property), to give private firms the right to employ up to 40 people and reduce tax rates to non-punitive levels. For firms in the public sector, the power of the planners is to be reduced by ending Five-Year Plans and reducing the number of plan indicators by perhaps as much as 90% from the current level of almost 700 (Planning Minister Dlouhy, as reported in *The Financial Times*, 18 January 1990). But the concept of the Plan remains.

Although these changes all point in the right direction, there must be a question-mark over timing. The experience of gradual reforms in Hungary and Poland is that they do not deliver the hoped-for result. The maintenance of trade and other monopolies will slow adjustment in state enterprises where action is most needed. This will be compounded by the slow unification of the exchange rate, which will penalize the traded-goods sector and reduce the incentive to foreign capital. And, at the extreme, delay could allow the managers in the state enterprises to argue change to a standstill. On a political level the force of public opinion which carried the main architect of reform, Mr Komarek, into the post of Deputy Prime Minister might dissipate as apprehensions about the costs of adjustment are allowed to grow. If Poland is the test-case of big-bang reform, Czechoslovakia seems to be setting itself up as the laboratory for gradual reform. Both approaches carry risks, but those in the gradual approach are possibly greater.

GDR

Change in the GDR was driven by labour outflow. This took place, at least partially, for economic reasons. However, in the press of events following the opening of the Berlin Wall, it was not until mid-January 1990 that statements as to the future of the economy began to emerge. But these themselves were overtaken. By February, the issue of how to staunch the outflow of people to the FRG had come to dominate economic debate. This culminated in the proposal for a formal monetary union between the GDR and the FRG which was put to Mr Modrow, the Prime Minister of the GDR, by Chancellor Kohl on 14 February 1990. Since monetary union is such a major step and at the time of writing is still under negotiation, the rest of this section is devoted to the general implications for the GDR of substituting the Deutschmark for the Ostmark in both the short and long term.

The underlying logic of monetary union is that the labour outflow will not slow, let alone cease, until the differential in real income between the GDR and the FRG is stabilized. The proposal to unify the Deutschmark and the Ostmark would stabilize one element in the relationship between incomes on both sides of the border. East German workers would no longer face the risk of a fall in their real incomes as a result of the Ostmark devaluing against the Deutschmark.

The crucial choice is the rate of exchange. The official exchange rate is one Ostmark to one Deutschmark. At that rate, East German average wage rates of around 1200 Ostmarks per month would convert to about half of West German rates, although taxes reduce the West German net wage advantage. However, the productivity gap is greater still. Thus, while a 1 : 1 exchange rate might slow the outflow of workers, it is likely that East German enterprises will be uncompetitive. The result will be high unemployment and an increased incentive to emigrate. Similarly, foreign firms will not be attracted to invest in East Germany, thus slowing the adjustment process further.

If the rate is set low enough (and unofficial rates in February 1990 were around 6 Ostmarks to the DM, the official tourist rate was 3 : 1 and an official debt transaction took place at 2.5 : 1) to maintain the viability of East German enterprises and to attract capital, the impact on wage rates would be catastrophic. At 6 : 1 the East German monthly wage becomes DM 200, or less than a tenth of FRG levels. Once prices started to move to West German levels, the impact on real incomes would be even worse. The conclusion is that, if complete labour market integration were to take place, the maintenance of the labour force in East Germany would require either subsidies to capital, if the rate were too high and factory closures followed, or subsidies to labour, if the rate were too low for workers to stay.

This is not a problem faced by other East European countries. First, labour mobility is not complete – language, cultural and skill barriers exist – so that they are not under the same pressure as the GDR. Secondly, they have the opportunity to change their exchange rate if the rate is wrongly chosen and their industries are not competitive in world markets. In such circumstances, they also have an independent domestic macroeconomic policy which will allow them to tackle the inflationary implications of devaluations.

So what are the advantages of currency unification for the GDR? The first is that it could bury its macroeconomic problems in the larger German economy. Its debt would disappear in the FRG's net credit position, and its balance-of-payments deficit would be absorbed by the FRG's surplus. The anti-inflation credibility of the Bundesbank and exchange-rate stability would attract foreign capital. The GDR would be preferred to other East European countries, where devaluations could destroy the value of assets in the long term. It would also give immediate and free access to FRG capital markets.

Finally, unification of the exchange rates will force the pace of economic reform in East Germany. If the exchange rate cannot change, then the prices of labour and capital must respond quickly to changes in economic conditions. As may have become clear, the choice between faster and slower adjustment is not an easy one to take. There are potential costs and benefits to both options. Currency unification, however, forces East Germany to go down the fast route.

References

Hillman, A.L. (1990). 'Macroeconomic Policy in Hungary and its Macroeconomic Implications', *European Economy*, May.

Newberry, D.M. (1990). 'Tax Reform, Trade Liberalization and Industrial Restructuring in Hungary', *European Economy*, May.

Szalkai, I. (1989). 'The Elements of Policy for Rapidly Redressing the Hungarian Balance of Payments', *European Economy*, May.

5
HOW DOES THE SOVIET UNION FIT IN?

Neil Malcolm

This chapter addresses two main questions. First, how different is the USSR from the smaller East European countries, and how far can we treat it in the same way as them? Second, what part is the USSR likely to play in the region in the near future, and how are the West's actions likely to influence its behaviour?

The Soviet Union – a special case?
The Communist Party of the Soviet Union, unlike its counterparts in the other Warsaw Pact states, gained power through its own efforts. It has not had the burden of heading a regime perceived by the population as imposed from outside. It has managed with some success to identify itself with the nation, so far as Russians, and probably many Ukrainians and Belorussians, are concerned. The Soviet Communist Party has the further advantage of having ruled the country for over 70 years. During that time it has shaped social attitudes and patterns of behaviour in a way which makes the kind of sudden, all-embracing change seen in some of its western neighbours seem unlikely. There is a large, resourceful group – loosely referred to as 'the bureaucracy' – which has a vital interest in the perpetuation of a system whereby it controls all economic and political decisions. The richness of the USSR's natural resources and

the relative isolation of the mass of the population from foreign influences also help to explain why the process of change in the Soviet Union is lagging behind that in the East European states.

It is becoming clear, moreover, that whereas the process of 'de-Leninization' may in some cases traverse common stages – and here it has at times been possible to draw comparisons between Gorbachev and predecessors like Dubcek and Kadar – it is not a smooth, controllable process with a predictable outcome. Revolutionary events in Eastern Europe are spurring on radicals in Moscow while simultaneously increasing conservative determination to halt the reform process before it runs out of control. There is every prospect that the conflict will continue to cloud the outlook for some time. In the new, more democratic political atmosphere, an important part of the battle is the struggle for public opinion, and its outcome is by no means certain. Doubt is often expressed, for example, about whether the mass of the population will accept the changes associated with economic reform. There are indeed special cultural features which have to be taken into account.

It would be misleading to describe Russia as any less 'European' than, say, Romania or Bulgaria. It was cut off from the rest of the continent during the Middle Ages, but since the beginning of the eighteenth century it has been ruled by a succession of predominantly Westernizing regimes. Its intelligentsia has regarded itself, and has been accepted, as part of a European cultural community and has made a significant contribution to science and technology. It has played a key part in European international politics. Soviet Marxism-Leninism at one time provided the basis for an important continent-wide political movement. By the time of the 1917 Revolution, Russia was already the seventh industrial power in the world, and twenty years later Soviet industrial production had outstripped, at least in volume, that of all other European countries.

On the other hand, Russia does stand out, even in Eastern Europe, as a society where a Leninist, anti-capitalist regime was established before a commercial culture had time to develop properly. The state had been obliged to play an active role in building up the pre-revolutionary industrial base. Especially in the advanced sectors this industrial base was largely foreign-owned (and to a degree foreign-managed). Agricultural land was communally administered for the most part, which hampered the emergence of independent farmers. From 1929, the four-fifths of the population who lived on the land were conscripted into a centrally administered state and collective farm system.

It seems likely that the paternalistic bargain offered by communist states to their people – economic security, subsidies on essential goods and services and minimization of the most obvious social inequalities in exchange for an authoritarian political system – is more acceptable in most parts of the Soviet Union than it has proved to be elsewhere. For many Russians, it is argued, the arrangement is accepted as part of the natural order. They will find it very difficult to accept the idea of market pricing, of rewards for identifying scarcities, and of risk investment, or the appearance of a class of entrepreneurs. Any government which removes job security, withdraws subsidies, and exposes employees to exploitation by foreign capital will be regarded as irresponsible, possibly criminally irresponsible.

How far this assessment holds true in the Soviet Union of the 1990s is difficult to judge. After all, the parallel claim that decades of repression have thoroughly demoralized Soviet society and paralysed the capacity for political initiative has been abruptly disproved by the mushrooming of autonomous 'informal organizations' and proto-parties. Certainly, the cooperatives operating on market principles which were allowed to be established on a small scale from 1987 aroused enormous popular resentment, partly because of the (predictable) effects of their interaction with the price-controlled, shortage-ridden state economy – very high prices, illegal diversion of supplies, widespread criminality. Official figures gave cooperative prices in 1988 as three or four times higher on average than state prices, and earnings of their employees as almost twice those of state employees.[1] In the summer of 1989, striking workers regularly demanded the closure of cooperatives, and the experiment survived abolition moves in the Supreme Soviet in September by a narrow margin of votes.

Nevertheless, there is evidence that public attitudes are less clear-cut than this suggests. Reaction against the discredited centralized system seems to be playing an important part, especially among the younger generation. Public opinion polls in 1987 showed that support for the cooperatives ranged from 87% among those under 45 years old to 7.8% in the 61–75 age group. At the end of 1989, a survey of around a thousand inhabitants of Moscow showed that 62% of those aged 20–29 had 'a positive attitude' to the concept of profit (only 41% of the over-60s), and a majority of all age groups under 50 were in favour of allowing individual private enterprise.[2] In the current situation, where economic reform has not really made any serious progress, it seems that most people put the blame for shortages and price rises on privileged and incompetent 'bureaucrats'. This is an important factor behind the still over-whelming support for *perestroika*. How far such support will remain once the job losses, price rises and readjustment of wage relativities associated with genuine marketization begin to appear is a quite different question, but it would be simplistic to predict that it will vanish altogether. In the event that more authoritarian methods of pushing through reform had to be used, it is worth bearing in mind that among the most traditionally minded parts of the population, the habits of resignation and obedience to authority are particularly deeply ingrained – resistance might be weaker than is feared. There is no denying, of course, that there are deep-seated cultural obstacles to marketizing the Soviet economy: even in the best circumstances, the effects will be felt for decades.

The dilemmas of reform

Turning to the Soviet economy itself, we find again and again what are described in Moscow as 'problems of transition'. The intention is to replace one system by another. This cannot be done at a stroke, and yet changing individual elements one at a time may in many cases only make things worse. For example, the USSR has great difficulty in expanding its export capability in manufactures. Greater competitiveness will take years to achieve, which means that rouble convertibility and thoroughgoing liberalization of foreign trade cannot be contemplated in the near future. On the other hand, exposure to competition from abroad is envisaged as a key technique in the economic reform process necessary to build competitiveness. Another vicious circle involves the Soviet budget deficit, which from 1984 to 1989 rose from 11 billion to 120 billion roubles.[3] In January 1990 the Deputy Chairman of the State Statistical Committee estimated that there was 165 billion roubles of unsatisfied purchasing power in the economy (equivalent to 20% of national income).[4] Clearly, to free prices (which is the key to successful reform) in such circumstances would lead to a socially unacceptable level of inflation. Yet the budget deficit is provoked mainly by the need to shore up inefficient loss-making enterprises and only successful reform can remove that need. These two circles are linked, in so far as rouble convertibility is probably a precondition for setting up the kind of money market the Soviet government could use to lessen the inflationary effects of its budget deficits.

To break out of such a situation and first of all to reduce the chronic budget deficit needs subtle and flexible policies, determinedly applied. So far the picture has not been encouraging. The very high level of food subsidies, for example, has been repeatedly criticized by the Soviet leadership. Yet from 10 per cent of national income in 1986–7 they were forecast to reach nearly 14 per cent in 1989 (i.e. 88 billion roubles), and to rise again by 8 per cent, according to Finance Minister Pavlov, in 1990.[5] The Politburo clearly does not feel able to pay the political cost even of stabilizing the level of such payments. Strikes held in the summer of 1989 were typically settled simply by granting workers' demands for higher wages and better supplies. Now that censorship has been largely lifted, evidence is readily available in the Soviet press of a system reaching the limits of its capacity. The downturn in fuel and energy output brought the country close to a major power crisis in the winter of 1989–90. Environmental disasters are reported from all corners of the USSR. One leading agricultural specialist has warned of the possibility of famine conditions arising in 1990.

When we consider the infrastructure shortcomings – the road network is thin and poorly maintained (few routes are metalled outside the main urban centres), rail and air transport are overstretched, electronic communications are undeveloped – the skill shortages, particularly in the financial and services sector, and the lack of entrepreneurial talent, it becomes clear that there is no quick 'big bang' solution of axing subsidies and of comprehensive privatization, that the state will have to play an active, innovative part for some time. It will have to instil new practices of honest, competent public administration. It will need assistance from outside to cope with massive 'know-how' and training problems on a scale which dwarfs those in the small East European countries. There are apparently quick gains to be made by arranging the long-term leasing of collective and state farmland for private exploitation and by converting military production (a relatively very high proportion of Soviet output) to civilian purposes. But years of emigration and demoralization have left the countryside denuded of the kind of energetic labour force which is needed, and switching from weapons to consumer goods production cannot be done without large investment. In any case, neither project will work unless the overall economic framework is thoroughly recast. Yet plans for reform have been endlessly argued over and modified, and the nettle of decisive action has still to be grasped by the Soviet leadership.

Taken alongside the lack of clarity at the top level about what the end point of reform is to be, particularly in respect of markets for capital, this hesitancy suggests that the learning process is still incomplete. The unviability of the present system and of hybrid forms derived from it has not yet been thoroughly realized among influential groups. As things continue to deteriorate, of course, the choice will become clearer. In this sense, reform is inevitable sooner or later, but the later it comes the more difficult the process will be. As the examples of Poland and Romania show, change can be postponed almost to the point of catastrophe. In contrast to those East European countries further down the road of change, the Soviet Union is at an 'earlier' stage. The timetable and the exact path of reform are difficult to predict because of political considerations. It is particularly difficult to estimate how public opinion will react to increasing economic hardship, and how much resolution political leaders will display in forcing through necessary but unpopular policies. Special social/cultural features and the sheer size of the country mean that the scale of the task involved will, in any case, be much greater than elsewhere. The *prospect* of future large-scale Western assistance linked to genuine reform will be an important factor strengthening supporters of that reform inside the Soviet Union and speeding up its arrival. In the meantime, constructive steps can be taken. These will be discussed later in the chapter.

The Soviet Union in Eastern Europe

Moscow's new policy in the region
Another reason for finding ways, however small they may be, of strengthening supporters of economic reform in the USSR, and that includes the currently dominant faction in the leadership, is that at the present juncture economic reform, political reform and a reformed, non-interventionist Soviet policy in Eastern Europe go hand in hand. We shall look first at how and why this new policy

towards the region has emerged and then at possibilities for its development in the near future.

For many years, Soviet leaders kept close control over Eastern Europe, treating it almost as an extension of their own state. There have been three main justifications for this policy. First, the region was seen as a vital part of a 'world socialist economy' which it was expected would be able on the basis of internal specialization to outstrip the capitalist world. Second, it provided concrete evidence of the vitality and potential for expansion of the Soviet system and thus bolstered the domestic authority and foreign prestige of Soviet leaders. Third, it was perceived as an indispensable security asset, ensuring the permanent division of Germany and a buffer of 'friendly' countries between NATO and the Soviet border.

These three justifications for keeping a grip on the region have eroded one by one over the past two decades. Now only the third retains some degree of credibility among important groups in Moscow. The first to go was the idea that the Soviet Union derived, or was likely to derive, any substantial economic benefits from its association with the other European CMEA members. From the 1970s, there have been attempts to find ways of minimizing the burden of supporting these resource-poor, ineffective economies and to engage more actively in the world division of labour. In the 1980s, as the Soviet Union's own problems mounted and the technology lag widened, the benefits of relaxing constraints on East-West economic relations must have begun to seem more and more appealing. One of the earliest foreign-policy decisions of the Gorbachev administration, in 1985, was to restart negotiations between the EC and the CMEA. These had been blocked because of an earlier Soviet refusal to permit bilateral ties to be established between Brussels and the East European capitals. Such ties, it was claimed, were part of a plan for 'bridge-building' and subversion. Now Moscow accepted the Community's terms, encouraged Hungary and Poland to sign separate trade and cooperation agreements, and indeed signed one of its own, in Brussels in December 1989. A degree of differentiation in Eastern Europe, even when it was explicitly encouraged by EC spokesmen, was no longer perceived as a threat by Soviet leaders. It was becoming clear that the Community, with its rediscovered dynamism and its accumulated experience in international cooperation, would be the motor of economic integration, and growth, for the whole of Europe. If certain East European states were to become associated with it, this would open channels of communication, set precedents and generally make it less likely that the USSR itself would ultimately be excluded from the European recovery.[6]

By this time too the East European states were a poor advertisement for socialism, as economic problems and the political exhaustion of their regimes provoked demoralization, corruption and social unrest. This helped to strengthen doubts which were growing in the Soviet Union about the nature of the system which had been constructed. Under Gorbachev, specialists in East European affairs were in the forefront of those arguing that the 'command-administrative system' created by Stalin had reached a dead end and that the path to renewal led through democratization and marketization. They pointed out that if the coercive underpinning of 'democratic centralism' were to be removed in the USSR, the fraternal states of Eastern Europe could scarcely be denied the right of self-determination.[7] It is noticeable that the new approach to Eastern Europe began to be spelt out explicitly in 1987, just as the drive for democratization began to gather pace inside the Soviet Union. Thereafter it developed hand in hand, and came to fruition at the same time, in 1989.

It was inconceivable to *impose* a new, reformed system, since the Soviet reformers themselves had no clear idea of what it would be like. They, and Gorbachev after them, insisted that it was for the populations of the countries concerned to find their own solutions. It seems reasonable to suppose that few reformist Russians suspected how radical would be the solutions eventually chosen, the degree of Westernization and the political and security dilemmas which it would throw up. But even if they had foreseen the outcomes of 1989 and 1990, it is difficult to imagine what means of preventing them they would have seen as legitimate. In any case, the whole structure of thinking which counterposed Western and 'socialist' values in a black-and-white sense was now crumbling in the USSR. It was becoming quite acceptable to hold up social democracies such as Sweden as models from which lessons could be learned. The 'two camps' were coming to be replaced by a 'Common European Home'.

As for the security dimension, it was obvious that countries such as Poland were likely to prove unreliable allies in a crisis. Indeed, given the state of military technology in the late twentieth century, was there any security advantage in holding on to large tracts of 'buffer' territory in defiance of the wishes of the local population? It would surely be more logical to withdraw, and to try to salvage whatever perception of shared interests remained in the minds of previously unwilling partners, in the hope of building a genuine alliance. A powerful boost was given to this reappraisal by Gorbachev's new strategy of active diplomacy towards Western Europe and by the 'new thinking' realization that security was essentially a political matter – no nation could feel safe so long as it was seen as a threat by others. The large Soviet armed presence in Eastern Europe and its clumsily enforced hegemony, it was acknowledged, were insuperable obstacles to building relaxed and constructive relations with the west of the continent and hence with the West as a whole. To withdraw under the correct conditions would be a positive security gain.

The future of economic relations

The purpose of the Council for Mutual Economic Assistance (CMEA) was to foster 'planned' economic exchanges between the socialist countries. It never had a great deal of success; indeed, in so far as it formalized the state foreign trade monopolies of the participating states it was, and is, a hindrance to trade, which has over the years grown far more slowly in relation to national income than in Western economies of comparable size. Recently, moreover, East-West trade has been growing more quickly than East-East trade. In 1986, 1987 and 1988, for example, the USSR's exports to the market economies grew by 16%, 5% and 12% respectively by volume. The corresponding figures for its exports to the socialist economies were 6%, 1% and 1%.[8]

The CMEA is accordingly now being used as a forum to promote the idea of an East European 'common market' in which firms can exploit their new foreign trade rights to build a network of direct links. In January 1990 it adopted a policy that this trade should switch to a hard currency basis. In the broader European context, with cooperation agreements being signed and barriers being lowered between individual countries and the EC, current agreements do not imply a very ambitious degree of economic integration in the East. Indeed, although the weak bargaining power of the small, less-developed East European countries in relations with Brussels logically dictates a degree of cooperation and solidarity, this has not been forthcoming. There are widespread doubts concerning the very survival of the CMEA, in more than a purely consultative role.

It is difficult to see any change for the better in this respect occurring in the course of 1990. Indeed, intra-East European/Soviet economic relations are likely to deteriorate as the political reorientation to the West encourages the development of links across the board with countries like the FRG, Austria, Italy and France. New trade and cooperation agreements will be signed in Brussels, and national efforts will continue to be made to establish closer relations with the Community. At the same time, economic decline and dislocation will disrupt established ties, especially with the USSR.

In the rather longer term, however, other factors may stimulate the preservation of some kind of economic community among the countries of the region. The East European states export large quantities of low-quality manufactured and semi-manufactured goods to the USSR, and it is difficult to see where else they could sell them. In return, they have received essential imports in the form largely of fuels and raw materials. These can be obtained elsewhere, of course, but Moscow, if it wishes, can offer special prices, as it has done in the past, as a way of preserving ties. As more and more Soviet enterprises begin to exercise their rights to select their own trading partners abroad, many may prefer to go to Western and Far Eastern suppliers, but there will be strong political pressures not to let the process of fragmentation go too far too fast. 'Mexicanization' of the East European economies, it is claimed in Moscow, could encourage 'Balkanization' of international relations in general in the region, speeding up the erosion of the alliance system and creating dangers of instability and conflict.

Political-military relations
Until the summer of 1989, there was relative certainty about the limits of foreign policy change in Eastern Europe. In August of that year, Ronald Asmus was able to write that 'Soviet policy seems to amount to little more than one thick black line labelled geopolitical loyalty'.[9] Soviet reformers and East European leaders were careful to insist that while the new doctrine of self-determination implied the freedom to leave the Warsaw Treaty Organization, for instance, no one would feel inclined to do so, particularly as the mutual dismantling of military blocs in Europe was now on the agenda.[10] In

Poland, for example, foreign and security policy was deliberately excluded from the election campaign in the spring of 1989, and Solidarity publicly announced its acceptance of Warsaw Pact membership for Poland.

Soviet renunciations of the 'Brezhnev doctrine', which became increasingly unequivocal through the year,[11] and Soviet calls for the Warsaw Treaty Organization to become more 'politicized' (i.e. to build structures and procedures of consultation parallel to those operating in NATO), were clearly intended as a means of encouraging East European states not to leave the Pact. This is a major priority. In Soviet official statements in recent years, the emphasis has shifted away from the long-term goal of getting rid of the military alliances to the need for stability and continuity. In Strasbourg, in July 1989, Gorbachev declared: 'The present-day realities and prospects for the foreseeable future are obvious. The USSR and the USA constitute a natural part of the European international political structure.'[12] By the Malta summit in November, Gorbachev had stopped making any references to the dismantling of the blocs.

Soviet preoccupations have been to avoid what a leading reformist foreign policy expert in Moscow described as 'some kind of fusion which sweeps the east and west of Europe'. There is a fear that 'if the two Germanies immediately merge, the rest of Eastern Europe will be engulfed or devoured by the other side'.[13] These apprehensions are no doubt more keenly felt among the generation which remembers the experiences of World War II and among those directly responsible for national security. The prospect which is feared is of a sharp switch in the military balance of forces (in particular a sudden increase of German power) and of political isolation outside the boundaries of a 'greater Western Europe'.

Gorbachev's strategy for avoiding these outcomes is first of all to insist that troop reductions in Europe should be balanced and deep and should lead to non-threatening patterns of deployment on both sides, and to work for a new system of mutual security guarantees on the continent. In the second place, he pushes hard to increase the intensity of pan-European contacts in those institutions such as the CSCE (Helsinki process) which embrace the USSR, and to build links between the USSR and other European bodies like the EC and the Council of Europe. In the third place, he tries to preserve a political and military alliance in the East on terms acceptable to the other states involved, although as time goes by it appears less and less likely that such terms can be found.

The case of East Germany, where the military issue is most acute and where the reorientation towards the West will be swiftest, highlights Moscow's interest in speeding up the timetable of arms reductions envisaged in the CFE talks. This interest is encouraged by requests from the Czech government and from the Solidarity leadership in Poland for the withdrawal of the relatively smaller contingents of Soviet troops stationed there by the end of 1990, and by similar requests from the Hungarian government to withdraw by the end of the following year. Yet the real urgency is provided not so much by the prospect of Soviet withdrawals as by the gradual evaporation of any political rationale for the Eastern alliance and of any justification for counting, say, the 200,000-strong Czechoslovak armed forces on the 'Soviet' side.

The problem for the current administration in Moscow is that the process of social and political change in its neighbours to the west is running at a much faster pace than two other processes that must occur at the same time if its policy is to retain domestic support. The first of these is to construct a package embracing disarmament, military-doctrinal innovation, force restructuring and creation of a pan-European security system. Soviet spokesmen repeatedly state that any agreement on the future of Germany requires legal guarantees on borders in Eastern Europe, agreement on Germany's military status and on the future of the European alliance system.[14] This is a complicated task which will stretch well into the second half of the 1990s, even at an optimistic estimate. The second task, which is intertwined with the first one, is to bring about a thorough conversion to new thinking about European security issues among the Soviet military and other powerful elements in the Soviet foreign policy establishment. This is complicated, because there is no sign that NATO member states are in a particular hurry to withdraw their own troops stationed abroad. In the long run, Gorbachev may be able to defend to his voters the idea, say, that a small American presence in Europe is compatible with a complete Soviet withdrawal, in view of the USSR's greater proximity, but in the short term he will be faced with a Germany bent on reunification but with no desire for radical demilitarization. It will be a delicate matter to find a solution which is acceptable to both Germans and Russians.

Gorbachev and his colleagues have shown great flexibility on

European issues already, and they are undoubtedly ready to make further compromises if necessary. But they do face powerful political pressures at home, and they are beginning to approach the limits of domestic acceptability. In cases of breakdown in relations with the West, Gorbachev, or, more likely, a successor administration, would have sizeable traditional resources to fall back on if it felt it necessary to defend its position in, say, the key 'Northern Tier' states. Even after the 10% cut begun in 1989, Soviet forces in Eastern Europe will amount to 515,000, of which approximately three-quarters will be in East Germany. Even after the asymmetrical cuts which it is expected will be agreed in the CFE forum towards the end of 1990, and implemented by 1993 and 1994, Moscow will still have approaching 200,000 men in the region, concentrated overwhelmingly in Germany, backed up by immense military resources in the USSR itself. The presence of these troops is sanctioned by bilateral treaties, not by the Warsaw Treaty, and was originally agreed at the Potsdam conference at the end of World War II. In December 1989, the Soviet government repeatedly emphasized its rights 'as one of the Allied powers' to be consulted over the future of Germany. Of course, it is difficult to envisage the Soviet Union risking the severe political consequences of getting involved in coercive actions in East Germany. On the other hand, the theoretical possibility of this happening is a bargaining counter which could be used to achieve a more favourable settlement in the West, particularly with the Federal Republic. If expectations of unification are allowed to rise too high in the Federal Republic, Western governments fear its population may be tempted by a Soviet deal involving neutrality. There might also be opportunities for Moscow to play on Polish apprehensions about 'German revanchism', which are still lively, and on national rivalries and border disputes between other East European states.

Political uncertainties in the USSR

The 'overtaking' of the Soviet Union by reform in Eastern Europe increases political uncertainty in Moscow. The proclaimed rationale of *perestroika*, after all, is to *reform* communism. If it becomes clear that liberalization leads inevitably to the *rejection* of communism, Gorbachev's task of leadership becomes much more complicated. If radical political reform on the East European pattern, involving a sharp break with the existing system, were to occur in the near future in the Soviet Union, it would at first sight appear to simplify the West's calculations. However, at the current stage this might well prove to be a false dawn – a short diversion on the road to the other alternative to Gorbachevism, namely a more conservative, nationalist regime. Of course, even if it had the attention to spare from its internal problems, such a regime would be unlikely to attempt to reestablish control over Eastern Europe: it would undoubtedly meet damaging resistance in certain countries and it would incur enormous political, security and economic costs in its relations with the West. However, a less accommodating leadership could put at risk a number of benefits which Gorbachev's policy offers the West in the not too distant future, in particular, large-scale disarmament with disproportionate reductions on the Soviet side, and an amicable settlement of the German question which does not involve tempting the Federal Republic down the path to neutrality. In general, such a Soviet Union could intervene disruptively and to damaging effect in the international relations of Eastern Europe, relations which are likely to remain unsettled for some time.

How should the West respond?

In relation to the USSR, it must first of all be said that the fundamental factors of change are internal – the West can do only a limited amount to influence the outcome. However, it seems clear that the current administration in Moscow offers a better prospect than the conceivable alternatives for the kind of changes the West wants to come about in a lasting way – in the USSR, in East-West relations and in particular in Eastern Europe. It is misleading to portray Gorbachev and his supporters as men who are essentially determined to preserve a 'totalitarian' system at any cost. They have shown that they are prepared to go along – albeit step by step – with the logic of democratization, and have declared their readiness to accept the fundamental switch to a multi-party system.

In foreign affairs the Soviet President would be most threatened if his opponents could argue convincingly that his gamble on cooperation with the West had failed – that Western leaders were still prompted primarily by hostility to the USSR. Any moves which appeared to offer a frontal threat to Soviet security would be especially damaging: for example substantial increases in weaponry targeted at the USSR, or forwarding German unification in an unconditional way, unlinked to territorial and strategic agreements. Too high-profile an involvement in the domestic politics of East European states in the near future would be unsettling for similar reasons. Conversely, to cooperate in speeding up the disarmament process and perhaps to make some limited and non-disruptive but highly visible unilateral reductions would be helpful.

Because of its size and its lagging position in the economic reform process, and because of political uncertainties, the USSR is not, certainly at present, eligible for the kind of close relationship or even entry to the EC which is envisaged for some of the smaller East European countries. It is nevertheless important not to give the impression that the boundary of 'containment' has merely been moved a few thousand miles to the East, and that Moscow is being excluded from the world economic community which it is patently so anxious to join. Soviet formal ties with Western institutions such as the EC, the Council of Europe, GATT, the IMF and the World Bank are in many cases largely of symbolic significance, because of the practical obstacles at present to full participation, but they are none the less important for that. Such contacts could be broadened where feasible. A reappraisal of the dimensions and mode of operation of the COCOM system is overdue, especially in view of Moscow's new readiness to accept inspection and verification procedures. Otherwise there is a serious danger of sacrificing real long-term security to the shadow of short-term security improvements. Not just scientific and technological interests, but the whole range of educational and cultural links could be enormously expanded, at relatively small cost. This would permit a beginning to be made on infusing desperately needed 'know-how' and would strengthen Westernizing currents in Soviet society.

The Soviet government is no longer promoting pan-Europeanism and the 'Common European Home' as an *alternative* to NATO and to Brussels-centred integration but as something complementary to them. It seems to envisage a range of European institutions functioning in different spheres and helping to build closer networks wherever possible as opportunities arise. This seems an appropriate strategy to follow at a time of uncertainty about the future. The planned second phase of the CSCE could afford opportunities for exploring and promoting the common interests of the USSR and Western Europe in relation to Eastern Europe, especially in the area

97

of security, where a new agreement is urgently needed in order to compensate for the crumbling of the Warsaw Pact alliance. If this process is successful it will serve the additional common interest in advancing the institutionalization of relations between Moscow and the rest of the continent and eroding further the obsolescent psychology of confrontation which is still present on both sides.

Notes

1 *Izvestiya*, 28 October, 1989. A good brief analysis of the issues at stake in the Soviet economic reform is given in P. Hanson, 'Capitalism or socialism?', *Detente*, no. 16 (1989).
2 A. Aslund, *Gorbachev's Struggle for Economic Reform* (London: Pinter 1989), p. 172; *Moscow News*, 1990, no. 2. Public opinion polls in the Soviet Union are, it should be said, sometimes narrowly based and unreliable.
3 Central Intelligence Agency, *USSR: Sharply Higher Budget Deficits Threaten Perestroyka* (Washington, DC: GPO, 1988); R. Yur'ev, Raskryvaem tainy byudzheta', *Pravitel'stvennyi vestnik*, 1989, no. 18, p. 6; V. Pavlov, budget speech reported in *Ekonomicheskaya gazeta*, 1989, no. 40. This section draws heavily on D. Dyker, 'The Soviet Union', paper presented to the RIIA study group on 'Reform in Eastern Europe', December 1989.
4 Nikolai Belov, reported in *The Independent*, 26 January 1990.
5 Yu. Borozdin, 'Ekonomicheskaya reforma i tovarno-denezhnye otnosheniya', *Voprosy ekonomiki*, 1989, no. 9, p. 25.
6 N. Malcolm, *Soviet Policy Perspectives on Western Europe* (London: RIIA/Routledge, 1989), Chapter 5.
7 See for example the comments by Oleg Bogomolov, director of the Institute of the Economics of the World Socialist System, in *Sovetskaya kultura*, 12 July 1988, cited by R. Asmus, 'Evolution of Soviet-East European Relations under Mikhail Gorbachev', *Radio Free Europe Background Report*, 22 August 1989 (no. 153).
8 Economic Commission for Europe, *Economic Survey of Europe in 1988–89* (New York: United Nations, 1989), p. 159.
9 Asmus (above, n. 7), p. 11.
10 There were one or two notorious exceptions. At a Moscow press conference in the summer of 1989, Oleg Bogomolov declared that if Hungary, say, decided on neutrality, then nobody would stop it. Asmus (above, n. 7), p. 11, n. 34.
11 In Strasbourg in July 1989 Gorbachev stated: 'Any attempts to restrict the sovereignty of states, friends, allies or any others, are inadmissible.' *Pravda*, 7 July 1989.

12 *Pravda*, 7 July 1989.
13 Oleg Bykov, a deputy director of the Institute of the World Economy and International Relations, cited in *The Financial Times*, 24 January 1990.
14 Most recently, see Gorbachev's statement on 30 January 1990 acknowledging the inevitability of unification, and stressing the need to safeguard existing boundaries – 'There are two states, four-power obligations still exist, and there is the European process' – *The Financial Times*, 30 January 1990.

6

WESTERN POLICY: THE ROOM FOR MANOEUVRE

J.M.C. Rollo

The underlying assumption of this chapter is that the Western democracies, and the multilateral institutions which underpin the Western economic and political system, wish to encourage change in Eastern Europe. They wish to do so because such change would improve the long-term security and stability of Europe as well as increasing the liberty of those in Eastern Europe. Thus there is a commitment to long-term support for democracy and the construction of market economies. This may seem self-evident; but, as the costs of managing the transition in Eastern Europe become clear, these objectives may become obscured.

It follows from this formulation that it is essential to focus on the long term and not simply to muddle through one year at a time. It further follows that the key is structural policy – both politically and economically – and not just balance-of-payments support, no matter how important that is in the short to medium term.

What can Western countries do?
Perhaps the first thing that Western countries can do is to admit that they have no special wisdom about the process of transition. The problem of substituting democracy and a market-based economic system for a totalitarian one has not been faced anywhere before. The West does, however, know about some of the components and

100

objectives of change. That said, priority should be given to the issues identified in Chapters 2, 3 and 4. On the political side, these are:

- institution-building;
- party-building;
- advice on constitutional reforms and voting systems; and
- help with reforming central and local bureaucracy and introducing modern public-sector management methods.

On the economic side, the targets for action should be:

- short- and medium-term balance-of-payment problems;
- domestic macrostabilization policy; and
- help in setting up market institutions, such as capital markets, central banks, regulatory regimes and bodies, trade policy, labour market policy, civil legal systems and environmental policy.

The matrix shown in Table 6.1 is an attempt to identify the policy options and policy actors. Without much difficulty one can arrive at some 500 policy-choice/policy-actor combinations. Many of them are empty cells, but none the less there are 170 active combinations. Even that combines groups of policies – notably institution-building and economic reintegration. Nor are the policy headings any more than the most obvious.

Before we turn to an analysis of the policy menu, one point needs to be made. There are six multilateral organizations, seven if the EC is included, and a further grouping of twenty-four countries, the G-24, in our matrix. All of them are capable of more or less independent action. Within the countries two levels of government may be involved, plus a wide range of independent institutions, including enterprises, trade unions, banks, charities, churches, academic institutions. The scope for duplication, conflicting action and other forms of wasteful behaviour is enormous. The risks involved in wasting the time of the relatively small number of people who actually can change anything in Eastern Europe are high; there is a danger of bureaucratic fatigue in the recipient countries. The premium is therefore on coordination among the donors. This need has already been recognized by the allocation to the EC Commission of the coordination of G-24 aid to Poland and Hungary. But the problem is going to grow, and it may be necessary to create special coordinating agencies for both donors and recipients – rather after

Table 6.1 Western policy–choice matrix

	IMF	IBRD	IFC	Paris Club	GATT	UN	OECD	COCOM
Financial policies								
Short-term b-o-p aid	×							
Medium-term b-o-p aid	×	×						
Structural adjustment aid		×	×					
Project aid		×	×			×		
Debt				×				
Knowledge transfer								
Training	×	×	×			×		
Technical assistance	×	×	×		×	×	×	
Technology transfer		×	×			×	×	×
Institution-building								
Political								
Economic								
Micro		×	×		×	×	×	
Macro	×	×				×	×	
Policy advice								
Political								
Economic								
Micro		×	×		×	×	×	
Macro	×	×				×	×	
Environmental policy								
Policy advice		×				×	×	
Conversion costs		×	×				×	
Clean-up costs		×						
Private sector								
Direct investment			×					
Trade credits								
Official policies to encourage the private sector								
Investment protection			×					
Tax agreements								
Trade credits								
Economic integration								
Freedom of movement of:								
Goods					×		×	
Services					×		×	
Capital							×	
Labour						×		
Membership of multilateral organizations	×	×			×		×	
Political integration								
Membership of multilateral organizations								

b-o-p – balance of payments

European Community				G-24 countries					
				Government		Non-govt. organizations			
Gen. policy	EPC	Budget	EIB	Central	Local	Firms	Banks	Found- ations	Polit. parties
		×		×					
		×		×					
		×	×	×					
		×	×	×					
				×		×	×		
		×	×	×	×	×	×	×	×
		×	×	×	×	×	×	×	×
		×	×	×	×	×	×	×	
×	×			×				×	×
×			×	×	×	×	×	×	
×				×			×	×	
			×	×			×	×	
×			×	×	×	×	×	×	×
×				×			×	×	×
×		×	×	×				×	
				×	×	×		×	
		×	×	×		×			
			×	×		×	×		
						×	×		
×		×		×		×			
				×					
				×					
×				×					
×				×					
×				×					
×				×					
×				×					×
				×	×			×	×

the style of the OECD or the Marshall Plan. This point is returned to in Chapter 7.

The policy menu

Financial stabilization
The core of the problem in three out of the four countries selected for special study is accumulated debt. Czechoslovakia is not badly placed in this respect and can be left to the market for the time being. Similarly, East Germany's debt problem lies largely with the Federal Republic, and as such can be left to be dealt with against the background of the likely integration of the two economies. For the other countries what is required is a combination of short-term balance-of-payments support, medium-term balance-of-payments/structural adjustment lending and debt relief. All of these need to be applied in a policy framework which will shift resources into the balance of payments. This is a familiar problem of the 1980s, and there is a well-worked-out procedure, derived from experience in Latin America and Africa.

The key institutions are the IMF, the World Bank and the Paris Club. The IMF will make emergency credits available to bridge immediate financing gaps. These are forthcoming, however, only against a policy programme which the Fund's staff and Board of Directors see as attacking the underlying macroeconomic problems. Typically, a policy programme is required to include performance indicators that are intended to deflate domestic demand both by raising real interest rates and by balancing fiscal policy while depreciating the exchange rate. The negotiation of a short-term or Stand-By Agreement (SBA) with the Fund is doubly important. Without such an agreement the World Bank will not come forward with the longer-term programmes designed to improve the structure of the economy. These so-called structural adjustment loans usually amount to direct balance-of-payments support over three years, tied to reform of specific microeconomic policies, such as trade policy, agricultural policy, commodity tax policy, pricing policy and state enterprises.

An IMF programme also triggers debt-rescheduling. Sovereign debt is either government-to-government – usually aid loans and trade credits, both subsidized and unsubsidized – or commercial bank loans. These are dealt with in the Paris Club and the London Club respectively. These clubs exist to defend creditors from being picked off by the debtors. Equally, they allow coordination with the IMF teams negotiating with the debtor countries about short-term programmes.

Individual creditor countries also go beyond their involvement through the Bretton Woods institutions and the Paris Club. They may, because of historical or political links, offer aid in the form of grant or of soft loans to help bridge any remaining financing gap.

This last point brings us to an important distinction between grant and credits. IMF programmes are essentially overdraft facilities. They must be paid back – at broadly dollar rates of interest – within seven years. Similarly, the programmes of the World Bank – or, to give it its proper name, the International Bank for Reconstruction and Development (IBRD) – are 20-year loans at commercial, albeit very fine, terms. Debt-reschedulings are precisely that: they simply attenuate the debt-repayment schedule and offer new grace periods on interest. The net effect of these programmes is to increase the total indebtedness of the country and its eventual debt-service burden – an apparently paradoxical approach to solving a debt problem. The hope is, however, that a combination of policy changes and breathing-space will lift the country onto a higher growth path, which will allow it to service its higher debts comfortably. The condition for this is that the real growth of net exports of goods and services be higher than the real interest rate on debt. At this point normal commercial borrowing will return as an option. Examples of where this has happened are Japan and more recently South Korea, whose exports have been growing so fast that it could retire debt rapidly through the 1980s despite being considered a 'problem' debtor as recently as 1982. That is one reason for Western countries sticking with credits as the main approach; the other reflects the wider dynamics of the debt problem.

If the East European countries were the only problem debtors, one might take the view that the sheer stock of debt is such that there is no conceivable way in which it could be repaid. The best way out would simply be to forgive the debt and allow the countries to start again. The arguments against forgiveness are largely based on insurance concepts – notably moral hazard. Moral hazard is said to take place when the existence of insurance encourages the behaviour insured against. Thus, if bad policies are rewarded with debt-forgiveness, other debtors will follow that example, thereby setting up a potential risk to the commercial banking system worldwide. Up to now, such debt-forgiveness has been applied only in the case of the poorest African debtors, whose resource endowments are very low relative to the debt burden. For middle-income debtors the potential to grow out of the problem exists. The East Europeans clearly qualify as at least middle-income debtors.

That does not mean that there are not ways of reducing debt burdens. The most obvious is to take advantage of the low price of debt on secondary markets (Polish debt currently trades at 17% of its face value). Thus, by judicious borrowing and repurchasing, debt burdens could be reduced. Foreign governments could help by standing guarantee for the new loans. Of course any increase in demand for such debt would send up its price. Another approach, which can be combined with the above, is to swap dept for equity. Thus the risk on the debt is shifted from borrower to lender. This might also help to mop up the large quantities of hard currency circulating in some East European countries. Citizens could buy in foreign debt at a discount and exchange it for a share in domestic industry. Making such schemes work may be the only way of accessing new money from the commercial sector (already commercial debt represents 20% of the Polish stock of debt and 40% of East European debt as a whole).

Overall the main constraints on Western action on financial policies are:

- the general constraints on public expenditure that prevent grant aid;
- the potential problems of moral hazard in the debt field; and
- a perception that the macro economy/debt problems are essentially symptoms of a structural malaise which can be altered only by policy reform, private-sector skills and equity funds on commercial terms.

Knowledge transfer

As noted in Chapters 3 and 4, the chief asset of the East European countries, and in particular of the four taken for special study, is the potential of their labour force. Labour is educated but not trained, and is employed in structures which destroy the incentives to improve either the individual or the practice. Any response to this from the West must have a number of dimensions. The returns on this response are, however, potentially huge, so that it should form the core of any long-term approach to the problems of these countries.

In Table 6.1 this category is broken down into five headings: training, technical assistance (that is, sending Westerners to do specific jobs and to raise their own successors), technology transfer, institution-building and policy advice. Superficially these all appear to be in the public sector, but this need not be so. Much of training and technology transfer will come from job experience. This will be tied as much to private investment (see below) as to public-sector projects; indeed, to be successful, it will be tied *more* closely to the private sector.

Similarly, institution-building includes putting together a system of civil law which enables the private sector to function efficiently; setting up capital markets, notably stock markets and secondary markets in government bonds; and introducing regulatory systems which define the limits of the public sector and control private economic power. These will call on private-sector skills as much as public.

The constraints on Western action in this area are also less. As long as the incentives are right – and that largely depends on exchange rates and legal systems – private capital will flow to these countries, taking with it skills and technology. Similarly, human capital is relatively cheap. The cost of a team – even of highly paid central bank officials or legislative experts – is small compared with the cost of a road or a dam. Equally, training courses in private- and public-sector management techniques are not expensive to the West. The main costs may be in Eastern Europe; the cost of losing high-quality labour, for a year or more, may be high in the short term relative to any long-term benefits.

Private-sector action

This brings us to what is probably the central Western actor in Eastern Europe. It was governments which caused the East European economic catastrophe. Governments will remain import-ant in the transition from central planning to the market, but in the long run the private sector, and above all foreign capital, will also be necessary to the success of the process.

The key attraction for foreign capital will be the high-quality workforces available at low wages. The general collapse of exchange rates in Eastern Europe allows potentially very high profits to be made on foreign markets if modern techniques can be married with East European workers. Western firms will need reassurance that:

- real exchange rates will not be allowed to appreciate faster than productivity growth;
- profits can be remitted;
- there are, and will be, no current or future restrictions on their freedom to manage plants;
- tax policy is non-discriminatory and non-confiscatory.

These guarantees, plus the high returns, should unlock new flows of savings from the West.

The commercial banks, too, could help by offering commercial trade credits for these countries. This would encourage the purchase of modern technology. To the extent that the credits will facilitate Western exports to the new, potentially very profitable, indigenous private sector, they should be secure. However, against a background of debt-rescheduling, it will be very difficult to activate private-sector trade credits. Western banks and capital market institutions should also consider setting up venture capital funds as a means of revitalizing the East European private sector. This would avoid the problems of debt-financing. The risks, however, as with any equity investment, are higher.

Official support for the private sector

This is the most difficult area for Western governments to be effective in. The important choices must lie with firms and entrepreneurs. The case for public involvement in those choices is no longer taken for granted in the West: rather the opposite. As a result, public policies tend to be targeted on offsetting risk which the market might overestimate. The lack of direct public-policy leverage on private-sector involvement raises the question of how Western governments can improve the commercial environment in which the reformed economies will have to work.

The most obvious government-to-government policies are double taxation agreements and investment protection agreements (IPAs). Taxation agreements, in particular, are crucial to the profitability of overseas investments. Without them, firms may be forced into artificial arrangements which lead to incorporation off-shore. While there is nothing wrong in this in itself, it is an option more open to large firms than to the small or medium-sized, and may reduce the potential value of direct investment.

IPAs are a way of giving home governments a role in guaranteeing the security of an investment against host-government action. They are normally bilateral in nature. There may be less formal ways of increasing the security of investment, such as going into a country alongside investment from the multilateral agencies, notably the International Finance Corporation, which is the equity investment arm of the World Bank.

Public-sector trade credits and investment insurance schemes also have a role in boosting private-sector involvement in Eastern Europe. Debt-rescheduling problems, however, will reduce the enthusiasm of public authorities for extending trade credits on the necessary scale. Equally, an expansion of investment insurance schemes – which are relatively little used at the moment – would unbalance the risk portfolio of public agencies. East European membership of the Multilateral Investment Guarantee Agency (MIGA), which is sponsored by the World Bank, might increase the confidence of investors. However, the real risks in Eastern Europe are commercial rather than arbitrary government action.

Economic reintegration
Up to this point the discussion has been on how Western institutions can advance the economic reforms inside Eastern Europe. The long-term success of these reforms, however, depends on Eastern Europe having full access to the world economy. This is a much more sensitive issue because it raises the question of exposing Western markets for goods and factors of production to competition from Eastern Europe. That competition could be very severe. The effect of depreciating exchange rates by itself could give a substantial boost to East European competitiveness vis-à-vis low-cost producers in southern Europe and the newly industrializing economies (NIEs).

None the less, the openness of Western economies to goods, services and labour from Eastern Europe is the ultimate test of the West's commitment to the economic reform process. Without access, the process is a wasted effort. This applies particularly to the markets of Western Europe. These are the nearest, and hence the most natural, destination for East European goods. They are also traditional markets. The one proviso would have to be that the policies of Eastern Europe were themselves open or on a clear path to openness. As has been stressed, these are not less-developed countries for whom special treatment should be available. While that would give some privileges, it would allow them to maintain protectionist regimes and reduce their bargaining power in GATT negotiations or when faced with selective trade measures. That would risk repeating the mistakes of the CMEA, albeit in a milder form.

The degree of reintegration is potentially wide and the criteria for access to the various levels of reintegration vary. The first and lowest level at which the East European countries can be said to be integrated into the world market is through the Bretton Woods institutions and in particular membership of the GATT. Of the four, Poland and Hungary are members of the Fund, the World Bank and the GATT. Czechoslovakia has applied to take up membership of the Bank and the Fund, and to reactivate its membership of the GATT. Membership, however, is not enough. Those countries which are already members of the GATT, for example, have been so under the state-trading heading. That has reduced their bargaining power and they have been subject to quantitative restrictions (QRs), voluntary export restraints (VERs) and anti-dumping actions, which have restricted their ability to trade.

The first moves are being made to open up trade. The EC trade agreements with Poland (19 September 1989), Hungary (26 September 1988) and Czechoslovakia (19 December 1988) have already accelerated the removal of QRs and the move to most-favoured-nation (MFN) treatment. The US and the rest of the G-24 have given similar treatment. The EC has given, and others are considering offering, General System of Preferences (GSP) treatment to East European countries. While the GSP offers tariff-free entry on a range of products and hence may improve short-term access, the longer-term implications are not good. There is often a quota on the quantities eligible for the tariff concession. The concessions are often available only on goods at the lower end of the value-added spectrum, thus tending to freeze production structures there. More insidiously, GSP implies that the recipient is not a fully functioning member of the world economy and requires special help. By itself, this may not necessarily be a bad thing. It does, however, tend to weaken the bargaining position of the recipient if the donor introduces selective and protective measures against products not covered by the GSP.

More generally, a successful conclusion to the Uruguay Round of trade negotiations would improve the value of GATT membership substantially. It would open up markets in agriculture and textiles, give more discipline over measures such as VERs, regulate trade in services, reduce tariffs and generally increase the comeback of the smaller members against the larger by improving dispute-settlement procedures.

Beyond the multilateralism of the GATT, more intense forms of integration are available on a regional basis. Superficially, the most obvious is to build on previous CMEA links to create a customs union, or common market, based on common tariffs and regulatory frameworks (see below for definition). The advantages of this are hard to see. To integrate, behind protective barriers, economies which are already deformed by past mistakes might give some gains in economic efficiency over existing structures and could increase bargaining power. But, depending on the degree of external protection, regional integration would probably merely serve to preserve the essentials of current structures of production and consumption. It would need to be very carefully designed if benefits were to outweigh costs.

Integration into wider European structures is the next category in the range. The large size of the European economy and its relative openness would give some guarantee of real competitive pressures as a result of opening up towards the rest of Europe. There are a number of possible institutional approaches, ranging through free trade areas, customs unions, common markets, currency union to monetary and economic union. The economic aspects of these are relatively easy to set out, as are the interests of the East Europeans in each category. The political and institutional implications are much more complex, not least because there are existing examples of free trade areas, customs unions, common markets and varying degrees of currency integration. Moreover, the existing institutions are in the process of changing. Superimposing the emerging countries of Eastern Europe on top of these processes of change would complicate already difficult negotiations.

It might be helpful to state the interest of East Europeans in each of these processes before examining the constraints on Western

111

responses. The first, or lowest, level of integration is a free trade area, which is an agreement between partners to remove all tariffs on trade between them in a specified range of goods while leaving existing tariffs in place against third parties. This is the initial approach taken by the European Free Trade Area (EFTA), both between members and (since 1972) between individual EFTA members and the European Community. These agreements are restricted to industrial goods. The appeal of this approach to the East Europeans would be in its simplicity. There is no very complicated institutional structure and little given up by way of effective decision-making. There is no need to change tariffs against third countries, for example, and no need to accept other countries' protectionist policies in exchange for access to their market. The disadvantages are that such an arrangement may not cover the full range of traded goods and services (agriculture – but not fully – and all services are excluded from EFTA), and it gives no presumption of protection against the use of selective trade measures such as VERs or anti-dumping actions.

The next step in increasing integration is a customs union. Here the members agree not only to free trade between themselves but also to a common tariff against third countries. There are gains in this approach, since the common external tariff prevents the need to guard against the potential for artificial trade flows in a free trade area where goods are imported through the country with the lowest tariff. More concretely, membership of a customs union would give the East Europeans the same guarantee that other members could not use selective protectionist measures against them. The other advantage for small countries is that they gain from the ability to use the combined bargaining power of the union in negotiations with third countries, e.g. in the GATT.

The disadvantages are, first, that the pooling of sovereignty with respect to trade policy against the rest of the world may lead to an increase in protection against third countries. Thus other parties may outvote them on issues of real domestic interest. Furthermore, on internal trade a customs union may replace transparently protectionist devices, for which there is redress in the GATT, with less transparent ones: subsidies for tariffs, competition policy for anti-dumping. Another disadvantage is that the product coverage of a customs union may be restricted. Thus products with complex domestic financial support policies – agriculture is the main example

– may be excluded because trade would undermine these policies. Equally, activity with complex regulatory regimes may be unaffected by tariff changes, e.g. pharmaceuticals. Services are also excluded. Finally, the lack of free movement of capital and labour may prevent economic efficiency being increased because these factors cannot move to areas where they could be best used.

The concept of a common market attempts to deal with these exclusions. It covers customs union for goods, rules about domestic subsidies, and regulatory regimes for goods and services and free market movement of capital and labour within the area. A perfectly functioning common market thus begins to come close to the ideal market. The bigger it is the better, since then it is more likely to include low-cost producers. Equally, the lower the external protection, the better. The advantages of such an approach for the East Europeans is the access it gives them to West European markets for goods, services, capital and labour. The loss of sovereignty is equally real because of the extent to which central institutions are required to administer integrated policies in a common market.

Monetary integration is also an available option. This could take a number of forms: from an unannounced link to a strong currency (say, the DM) through a formal link with margins of fluctuations – such as the exchange-rate mechanism (ERM) of the European Monetary System (EMS) – to immutably fixed exchange rates as in the Belgium/Luxembourg union. For the foreseeable future the East Europeans are likely to need considerable room for manoeuvre on exchange-rate policies if competitiveness is to be maintained.

Overall, the needs of the East Europeans might be best served by integration in a large open market for goods, services, capital and labour, with guarantees against selective protection. This would increase the credibility of market reform policies both at home and abroad, and bargaining power with respect to third countries. It suggests that membership of the European Community in economic terms – particularly once the 1992 process is completed – would offer a considerable advantage to the reforming countries. On the question of timing it is not easy to see major advantages to delay. The reforming countries must in any case make radical changes in their economic structures. If membership is an objective, it would be wasteful to go through an intermediate stage. The analogy with Spain and Portugal may thus be weak and the need for a long transition to full EC membership not proven.

The attractiveness of the EC option would be much reduced if monetary integration became a formal aspect of membership. In these circumstances something less than full membership but including the four freedoms of movement of goods, services, capital and labour would be attractive. This is in principle the arrangement which the current members of EFTA are negotiating with the European Community – although in that case it does not include a customs union.

The constraints

The constraints, however, are real. On the question of enlargement the EC has applications on the table from Turkey and Austria. The initial response to these is that they cannot be considered until 1993, when the unification of the markets of the existing twelve members is completed.

If the EFTA/EC negotiations fail to agree on an institutional structure for extending the four freedoms across both blocs, a number, perhaps most, of the members of EFTA may apply for full EC membership. That would be a major step for the Community and would raise large questions about its future structure (Wallace, 1989). To try to absorb the East-Central Europeans (and the Balkans in due course), with their economic structures in transition and their lower standards of living, is difficult to contemplate. The prospect of managing a community of up to 25 states, all at different levels of economic development, is daunting.

The difficulty facing the EC is that the special status of the GDR vis-à-vis the Federal Republic may short-circuit the whole process. As East Germany becomes a member through full political unification with the FRG, it may open the door not just to applications from the rest of the East Europeans but to others as well. It could also change the political conditions which are relevant to EC membership.

If full membership is not acceptable in the short term and EFTA members are reluctant to include the East Europeans in any arrangement that they may reach with the EC over the four freedoms, what is left? There is a tradition of association agreements, or way-stations, as Helen Wallace (1989) calls them, on the route to full membership (Turkey, Greece, Cyprus; see Wallace 1989) which might provide an answer. These include customs unions (excluding agriculture) but make no provision for services, capital or labour. They might offer some benefits against Community use of selective trade policy, and they would offer the vision of full membership eventually.

However, the experience of Turkey is not encouraging on either front. Moreover, the association agreements give none of the direct political benefits of full membership, such as the guarantee for democracy offered both by the conditions of entry and by the existence of an elected European Parliament (although there are alternatives, such as the Council of Europe, which has exerted some pressure on Turkey in the past).

Conclusions

The preceding analysis has highlighted three main constraints on action by the West to support economic change in Eastern Europe. The first is the practical difficulties that governments face in encouraging private capital to go to Eastern Europe. Since private capital is the key to sustaining the reforms in Eastern Europe, it will be largely up to the East Europeans to make policy changes that attract such capital. The second constraint is the difficulty in offering any long-term relief for public-sector debt. And, finally, the third is the pressure which governments are likely to encounter from domestic industries, and from selective trade measures, such as VERs or anti-dumping duties, that could be used against East European exports. Closer contact with, and finally perhaps membership of, the European Community seem the most obvious solution to this last danger. The economic benefits are there, but the constraints are enormous.

References
Wallace, H. (1989). *Widenening and Deepening: The European Community and the New European Agenda*, RIIA Discussion Papers 23, Royal Institute of International Affairs, London.

7

THE ROLE OF THE WEST

J.M.C. Rollo

Earlier chapters have argued that the end of Leninism in Eastern Europe and the consequent move towards market structures demands democracy. Equally, the analysis so far gives no credence to the view that there is a 'third way' between capitalism and socialism. If the legitimate aspirations of the peoples of Eastern Europe for a decent standard of living are to be met, then a market economy is necessary. Without a successful economic reform democracy may not survive. Thus democracy and economic reform are closely linked. Western support needs to continue to be conditional on both democracy and progress towards a market economy. That begs the question of how that conditionality can be sustained – a subject dealt with later in this chapter.

The second point that emerges from the analysis in earlier chapters is the enormity of the task and the lack of any usable blueprint from previous experience. There are examples of large and eventually successful macroeconomic stabilizations (Chile) but not in circumstances where there are no effective market structures or institutions in place. The problems facing Yugoslavia are instructive. There are examples of large-scale structural reform (New Zealand) but none of the degree required in Eastern Europe. There are even examples of a combined and massive macroeconomic and structural reform (Germany in 1948) but only where basic market structures were already in place and active. Such experience as we

116

have suggests, further, that these processes are usually more protracted and less immediately successful than was expected. The experience of Latin America in the 1980s does not give any confidence in quick solutions with predictable outcomes. Germany did not make an overnight adjustment in 1948; it was probably not until 1953, when the US and Britain forgave certain debts, that the success of the German reforms was guaranteed – and only after a number of crises. The next decade will be difficult and unpredictable for Eastern Europe, and Western support must be long-term and adaptive.

The underlying problem is broadly the same in each country, but there are differences in the degree and speed of reform required. At the same time the large number of institutions which could contribute from the West suggests a problem of coordination. Aid must be differentiated according to recipient and coordinated among donors.

Finally, it is worth remembering the sheer scale of this problem and the amount of savings that must be mobilized. The vast majority must come from the private sector in the country concerned and from Western capital markets. There is not enough public money in the West to match the scale of the problem. Western public policy towards the East Europeans must be aimed at mobilizing the private sector, not substituting for it.

Priorities for the West

Macroeconomic measures
Correcting macroeconomic imbalances is the area in which Western governments and public-sector institutions have their most obvious role. The short-term stabilizations in Poland, Hungary and the GDR are a priority requirement; immediate contributions, both through the IMF and bilaterally, are already being made in Poland and at the time of writing are planned for Hungary. The case of the GDR is special and is discussed below.

The longer-term debt problem remains. This has been partially recognized by the official creditors (the Paris Club), who have offered a 100% rescheduling of Polish public-sector debt (80% of the total) over the 13 months to March 1991, when the current IMF agreement ends. Thus, $9.5 bn of existing debt and service will be capitalized. The real benefit of this is doubtful, since it is unlikely

117

that in the absence of an IMF programme and supporting policies the loans would have been serviced.

The Hungarians face worse problems, since debt in Hungary is larger proportionate to GNP than in Poland. The long-term debt problem is therefore real, and if new foreign savings are to be tapped successfully, either growth has to be shifted onto a much higher plane than hitherto or old and unproductive debts must be reduced to make way for new productive borrowing. The difficulty is that a high growth path requires a net inflow of foreign resources, and that is unlikely to happen while the costs of servicing existing debt remain so high. Total rescheduling would give a breathing-space, but it is unlikely by itself to allow growth of output and exports to reach the necessary levels to attract new money in sufficient quantity. If the West is seriously committed to a long-term approach to change in Eastern Europe, it must find a way of reducing the stock of East European debt to manageable levels. If this can be done as a way of rewarding successful policies, it might avoid the moral hazard problems outlined in Chapter 6.

Structural measures

The West's primary long-term economic aim must be to help promote a market-based economy. As argued in Chapters 2 and 3, this requires not merely the freeing of prices but also the presence of legal and other institutions which will ensure that signals from free prices are not distorted. These necessary reforms include the establishment of property rights, a civil law covering contract, bankruptcy and accountancy standards, competition policy, trade policy and social welfare provisions.

The second major priority is to improve the efficiency of existing resources – above all labour, but also capital where it can be salvaged. That demands the training of personnel, the transfer of new technology and an increase in foreign direct investment.

The third priority is to open Western markets for goods and services to the East Europeans. The commitment must also be to maintain openness in the face of increased competition from the East. Western governments must be willing to face up to domestic producer lobbies. Western countries should also consider giving accelerated access in sectors where progress in the Uruguay Round of multilateral trade negotiations is likely to be slow, above all textiles and agriculture. Western capital markets should also be open to the East Europeans. There should be no differential restraints on prudent lending to these countries. Finally, the West should consider its policy on migration. The labour forces of the East European countries are their great asset. In the early stages of reform there will be considerable adjustment in employment levels and patterns; access to Western labour markets would provide an important safety valve. It would also provide a source of foreign exchange as workers remitted earnings to families at home. In the longer term it would provide a source of new skills, technology and capital as workers returned from the West.

Priorities among recipients and action to date

POLAND

Poland is the country where Western policy is most developed. The immediate priority must be to ensure that the stabilization programme undertaken by the Polish government is successful. That means backing the IMF programme with immediate injections of foreign exchange. As Table 7.1 shows, the West has made around $1 billion immediately available to increase reserves and stabilize the zloty at the new official rate of $1 = 9500 zloty. The approval of the IMF programme on 5 February 1990 in turn activated a 100% rescheduling of official debt by the Paris Club on 16 February 1990. This reduced capital repayment by around $9 billion (in the 13 months to March 1991). The World Bank is aiming to provide funds over the next three years amounting to $2.5 billion, tied to project and policy reform. These elements of balance-of-payments support were preceded by a programme of food aid amounting to some $400 million, mainly on grant terms, disbursed in late 1989 and 1990.

The other major elements of financial help also reflect the priorities spelt out above. Technical assistance and vocational training schemes have attracted specified grant aid in 1990 of around $170 million from nine countries. Almost all of the other G-24 countries have promised unspecified amounts of grant aid for training. In the field of encouraging investment there is a further $700 million available in the form of grants, loans or guarantees. At the same time export credit ceilings have been increased by around $3000 million, of which almost half is from the FRG. There is also project

Table 7.1 G-24 financial support committed to Poland as at
February 1990 (1990–5)

	mecu	$m	Status
Emergency food supplies	380	415	Mainly grant
Technical assistance to agriculture	20	22	Grant
Vocational training	158	170	Grant
Investments, joint venture and industrial development credit	640	700	Mixed grant and loan
Environment	93	100	Grant
Energy	27	30	Grant
Medical science and technology	16	17	Grant
Export credit guarantee ceilings	2850	3100	Guarantees, some to both Hungary and Poland
Project financing	3650	4000	Loans, some for both countries
International trade and investment insurance	320	350	Guarantees
EC Action Plan	2150	2350	Grant, includes aid for other E. European countries
Stabilization Fund	920	1000	Loan
IMF credit	644	700	Credit

Sources: Commission of the European Communities, Summary prepared for
PHARE meeting, December 1989; speech by Prime Minister Kaifu, Berlin, 9 January
1990; *The Financial Times*, 23 February 1990.

financing, mainly from the European Investment Bank (EIB), the IBRD and the EC but including some bilateral aid. This amounts to some $4000 million, but of this $1500 million is part of a pool available jointly to Poland and Hungary.

On trade opportunities, the EC-Poland agreement of September 1989 offered Poland full most-favoured-nation (MFN) status, abolition of quantitative restrictions and some unspecified General System of Preferences (GSP) concessions. A number of other G-24 countries also offered MFN treatment, and the US, Japan, Canada and Australia are considering offering GSP status. However, some quantitative restrictions against Poland remain, and protection against agriculture and textiles is still high. More dynamically, there is no guarantee that selective trade measures will not be used against Poland should the competitive pressures on G-24 markets become too great.

The immediate response of Western countries has broadly followed the objectives outlined earlier in this study. The main missing element is the lack of explicit long-term commitment. This shows up most notably in the lack of any action on debt relief beyond rescheduling; the restricted value of the trade agreement, which does not cover agriculture, textiles or services and gives no guarantees against the use of selective trade measures; and the lack of any recognition that labour migration may have a role to play in the process of reform.

Debt is a problem for the Paris Club. It would improve the chances of success of the Polish reform programme if, following the rescheduling of current debt, the Club could consider how good policy performance by Poland could lead to more permanent debt relief. A team of officials has been set up to consider longer-term aspects of Polish debt management. But the need is urgent. The unsustainable nature of the Polish debt burden and the probable disincentive effect it will have on private inward investment flows demands a response.

On trade and factor market issues, the focus is largely European for reasons of proximity. In terms of economic size, the most important actor is the European Community. While on political grounds the prospect of Polish membership seems distant, the economic benefits are important for the sustainability of economic reform. The Community needs therefore to consider closely whether there are intermediate arrangements which would give the Poles the main benefits of the four freedoms of movement of goods, services, capital and labour. At the very least the Commission should be giving the Poles detailed advice on how to construct regulatory regimes for goods and services which are consistent with the various regulations and directives under the 1992 process. It would be foolish to allow the Poles or others to build domestic regimes which were incompatible with those of the EC merely because of the need to delay any eventual membership process. The Community should also consider ways of giving Poland access to EC agricultural markets.

Statements by Commissioner Andriessen on possible Association agreements (Communication to Foreign Affairs Council of 5 February 1990) give no indication that the Commission has grasped the importance of either liberalizing beyond the current trade agreement or encouraging the Poles to base their regulatory structures on EC models.

HUNGARY

In general the priorities for action in Hungary are the same as those for Poland, but the emphases are different. The short-run macroeconomic problem is not as bad as in Poland, although the scale of the debt problem is proportionately greater (see Chapter 3 for details). The process of structural reform is further advanced. More of the necessary laws are in place than in Poland, rudimentary capital markets exist, and there is some equally rudimentary unemployment insurance. There are, however, changes that still need to take place. Currency convertibility remains limited, thus restricting the extent to which signals from the world market are passed through to firms and consumers. Trade policy is still restrictive, allowing monopoly to continue and slowing adjustment. The level of subsidies is too high, and the continuing lack of separation between monetary and fiscal policy results in continuing inflationary pressures.

The immediate policy objective should be successful implementation of the programme agreed at the end of February 1990 and approved in March 1990. This would help to accelerate the reform programme already under way and increase the attractiveness of Hungary to private capital, which must be the key to its long-term success.

The existing G-24 programme is largely focused on vocational training, investment and joint ventures, project financing and export

Table 7.2 G-24 financial support committed to Hungary as at February 1990 (1990–5)

	mecu	$m	Status
Vocational training	106	115	Grant, some for both Hungary and Poland
Investments, joint ventures	27	30	Grant
Environment	23	25	Grant
Energy	27	30	Grant, both Hungary and Poland
Export credit guarantee ceilings	1640	1785	Guarantees, some for both Hungary and Poland
International trade and investment insurance	185	200	Guarantees
Project financing	1085	1180	Loans, both Hungary and Poland
EC Action Plan	2150	2350	Grant, including aid for other E. European countries
Stabilization Fund	370	400	Loan
IMF credit	190	210	Loan

Sources: Commission of the European Communities, Summary prepared for PHARE meeting, December 1989; speech by Prime Minister Kaifu, Berlin, 9 January 1990; *The Financial Times*, 23 February 1990.

credits (see Table 7.2). Vocational training attracts specified commitments of over $100 million from six countries, and a further ten have offered unspecified amounts. Grant aid for joint ventures amounts to $30 million, a share of the $3,500 million available jointly to Poland, Hungary and other East Europeans from the EC and others for project finance, as well as part of the $2,500 million the World Bank is making available to Eastern Europe apart from Poland.

The trade access improvements on offer are the same as those for Poland except that the US has not yet granted full MFN status. They suffer the same drawbacks in as much as there are no guarantees against the reintroduction of selective protection. The Commission's offer of Association agreements suffers from the same disadvantages as for Poland.

The main improvements in Western policies towards Hungary would be, as with Poland, to increase the long-term continuity of commitment built into them. This could be achieved largely by debt relief, which would be conditional on policy improvements and a stronger arrangement with the Community covering trade in goods (including agriculture) and services, capital and labour, and by help in designing regulatory regimes for goods and services markets that are consistent with EC regulations.

CZECHOSLOVAKIA

As Chapters 3 and 4 make clear, Czechoslovakia starts with the blessing of not having a serious balance-of-payments or inflation problem to deal with. Neither does it have a debt burden of great significance ($7 billion, 5% of GDP, and a debt-service ratio of around 18%). Thus the priority in Czechoslovakia is to build on the economic reform process begun cautiously in early 1989.

A priority for the West must be to improve information on the Czech economy. That calls for rapid progress on Czechoslovakia reviving its relationship with the IMF, the World Bank and the GATT. The OECD and the EC Commission should also be closely involved, the former because of its background in structural reform issues, the latter in its G-24 coordinating role.

The emphasis should not merely be on macroeconomic statistics; information is also needed on the micro economy and the underlying incentive systems and competitive structures. Without such information it will be difficult to encourage those reforms which will lead to a stable market economy based on free goods and factor markets and the ownership of property.

Early priorities for Western support should be currency convertibility and an open trade policy. Following that, the priority should be to ensure that the legal reforms before the National Assembly institutionalize the right to own property and the setting up of a system of commercial law. The formation of capital markets should also be an early priority, since without capital markets the transfer of ownership necessary to ensure good management of existing and new resources will be impossible.

Western capital markets will also be crucial to Western private-sector involvement. Czechoslovakia's apparently good debt position should allow rapid expansion of lending both to back projects and to fund imports. Western governments and central banks should give clear guidance on the likely prudential limits to such lending to Czechoslovak institutions so as not to inhibit lending unnecessarily.

Finally, Western trade regimes should be made as open as possible, conditional on Czechoslovakia taking up its full responsibilities in GATT.

GDR

Although many of the economic problems in the GDR are similar to those of the other countries studied, the key issue is the relationship with the FRG. The GDR has high debts, a hard-currency deficit on the current account of the balance of payments, suppressed inflation, low productivity and a distorted production structure. The solutions to these problems are made both easier and more difficult by the relationship with the Federal Republic. The political demand for unification from within both parts of Germany is clear; the movement of people from the East to the West makes it inevitable. For the longer term, the ability of the GDR simply to change to FRG laws, to have access to FRG, and hence world, capital markets, and to lose its macroeconomic problems in the greater Germany all suggest that the transition to a functioning market democracy will come about much more rapidly than in other East European states.

As noted in Chapter 4, the main problem is a transitional one: how to manage unification in a way which reduces the outflow of young skilled labour to the FRG and begins to offer capital the incentive to move to the GDR. The key to staunching the outflow of people lies in setting out a credible path to economic and political unification – a process that may be easier on the political front than on the economic (see Chapters 2 and 3).

In any case, the short-term factors are largely economic. It is those with easily transferable skills who have been leaving for the FRG. This outflow will not slow until real income differentials (that is, wages and the prices of consumer goods) are stabilized and there is a prospect of the differentials closing.

The attraction of monetary union is that it begins the stabilization process by fixing the relationship between the two currencies irrevocably. However, as long as real wage differentials remain, there will be an incentive for workers to move to the FRG. The more so because, at any plausible exchange rate, East German wage rates are likely to be much less than half of West German levels. As prices of goods in East Germany begin to rise to West German levels (services may take longer), the real income will be lower still and the incentive to move greater.

Thus wages must be raised in the East. To do this without inflation, productivity must rise to West German levels, which in turn requires an injection of new capital, equipment, management and training. If the rate at which Deutschmarks are exchanged for Ostmarks is set low enough, existing firms will survive and private capital will be attracted but East German labour will wish to leave. If the rate is higher and labour is more inclined to stay, the less likely existing firms are to survive and the less attractive the GDR will be to Western capital.

The public sector will also have a role to play. To maintain a public-sector infrastructure in East Germany, teachers, doctors, nurses and local government officials will all require to be paid at rates similar to those in the West. But more may be needed. If, as noted above, the chosen exchange rate fixes East German wages at too high a level, the Federal government may need to pay subsidies to capital to go to the East. If, on the other hand, the wages are fixed at too low a level, the Federal government may be forced to pay subsidies to East German workers to stay. The alternative to those costs is also real, for there are immediate public-expenditure costs of East German refugees in the FRG. There might also be short-term inflationary problems, coming through the construction sectors in particular, as housing shortages develop in the FRG. In the longer term these refugees would cease to be a call on the public purse, and output in West Germany will be higher. The Eastern Länder, as they will have become, will have a low and ageing population and a poor industrial structure which will need continuing public expenditure. It might be better to use public money now to try to maintain the workforce in the East and encourage new high-productivity investment by subsidies to factors of production.

As part of that process the FRG will also have to provide the people and training required to replace existing legal and administrative structures with the FRG versions. It will have to find a way of transferring ownership of existing state firms and assets through capital markets to private ownership.

For obvious reasons, the management of the economic transition from two Germanies must largely be the task of the FRG among Western countries. The FRG is in any case best equipped to finance this transition; and, apart from the EC dimension, where there will be an impact on the Community budget through the extra costs of structural funds and agriculture (partially offset by extra budget contributions), the role of other Western countries lies primarily in managing the potential effects of unification on security and relations with the USSR.

THE SOVIET UNION

The process of change in the Soviet Union fits well into the framework set out in earlier chapters, and hence the needs of the Soviet Union as regards Western help are in principle similar to those of Eastern Europe. The main difference, as argued in Chapter 5, is the size of the problem and the presence of more entrenched Leninist structures which limit the scope of possible Western involvement in the near future. The other difference is that although the current leadership endorses the principle of multi-party democracy, there is still a great deal of uncertainty over the prospects and the timetable for political and economic reform.

The emphasis of Western policy should, as Chapter 5 concludes, be to stop the Soviet Union being and feeling isolated and hence threatened by events in Eastern Europe. It should also contain an element of progressiveness, so that any assistance given now contains within it the promise of further assistance as change goes ahead in the Soviet Union. Thus the starting-point would be reassurance on security issues through the CFE and CSCE processes. At the same time the Bretton Woods institutions and the OECD should form closer relationships with the USSR but falling short of full membership. This would allow the gathering and analysis of data on the Soviet Union, which in turn would encourage private-sector involvement. It would also give the Soviets access to advice on issues such as currency convertibility, the role of a central bank, the practice of fiscal policy, trade and competition, and industrial policy.

Trade links are another major area for Western action. The EC and the Soviet Union have already concluded a trade agreement. This does not yet go as far as the EC-Poland or EC-Hungary agreements. In economic terms there is no reason for not opening up completely to Soviet exports. It is true that the existence of a non-convertible currency and, for the moment, state subsidy raises the likelihood of distorted trade patterns. But that is not, by itself, enough to argue against unilateral liberalization. The real argument against equal treatment of the Soviet Union is political. Until the Soviet Union has moved as far as the East European countries, it should not be given equivalent access. Equally, close integration into EC structures must be avoided until democratic stability is demonstrated. The one area where the West can be, should be, and is moving is COCOM. A relaxation of restrictions on the 'mixed' list would do much to open up Soviet industry to new technology and production methods.

Policy coordination

The matrix in Chapter 6 (Table 6.1) gives a broad indication of the potential complexity of the Western contribution to change in Eastern Europe. Twenty-four governments, countless non-governmental institutions, up to seven multilateral agencies, combined with some 30 policy categories and up to eight target countries (including the Balkans and the USSR), all suggests a major problem of ensuring coherence and effectiveness for the West. Although official aid is likely to be less important than private-sector involvement over the long term, it will be more important in the short term. On the recipients' side, new governments, with inexperienced ministers and advisers who are already run off their feet, must face such diversity with sinking hearts. Perhaps once things settle down, ministers are in charge of bureaucracies, policies are beginning to work and people can relax, this degree of diversity will be less of a problem. Until then the strain that incoming visitors put on domestic administrations cannot be underestimated. Equally, the different identification, appraisal, conditionality and disbursement rules used by different donors, combined with different views on policy priorities (even within sectors), all add to the probability of confusion. The overall effect may be to reduce the efficacy of the Western effort and slow progress in the countries of Eastern Europe.

This point is already well recognized in other contexts. The IMF provides an analytical and policy framework within which balance-of-payments support can be assessed and disbursed without each contributing country negotiating a separate agreement. Equally, the World Bank has developed a parallel role on general structural policy aid and is setting up coordinating groups for aid operations in particular countries. These, however, still leave the recipient country bureaucracies facing a multitude of bilateral donors.

From the viewpoint of the recipient countries, the ideal would be for them to be left to disburse aid on their own responsibility, albeit within the objectives set by donors. For the donors, the history of overseas aid operations, and the domestic need to account for the use of taxpayers' money, demand a close control of funds. In a period of rapid change, however, such control may be illusory, its only result being delay and ultimately irrelevance.

This last point raises the question of what is meant by condition-ality and whether it can be obtained. It is the view of this paper and of all Western donors that aid should be forthcoming only as long as the recipients are pursuing the objectives of multi-party democracy and a market economy. The objective of multi-party democracy can be achieved within a variety of constitutional frameworks, but it is fairly readily recognized and is soon to be in place in the countries of Eastern Europe. The objective of progress towards a market economy is more difficult to assess. If the objective is that finally these states should be functioning market economies, it may be ten years or more before unambiguous success can be declared. If the objective is to set a programme for change with intermediate objectives, this will be subject to the pressure of events, and success will be equally difficult to assess.

This problem is illustrated by the discussion of privatization in Chapter 4. The different approaches may recommend themselves to different donor governments on the basis of their view of the role of the state. Those governments which take a restricted view of the role of the state may favour simply giving the state enterprises away to their existing workers. Other governments might be more sympathetic to equity arguments for distributing shares to everyone in the population. Yet others, for reasons of fiscal policy or practical considerations (pressure on capital markets), might prefer to take the process slowly and ensure that the proceeds accrued to the government (taking as an example British and Portuguese privatizations). There is no correct answer to these questions; the role of the state is a choice for the domestic electorate and not overseas governments. Thus it is possible that economic conditionality could undermine democratic structures by imposing the sort of outside control that was considered reprehensible under Soviet domination.

The difficulty of pursuing detailed conditionality leads to the question of whether conditionality is capable of being pursued at the level of the programme. Thus, as with IMF Stand-By Agreements, some central organization representing the donors would approve the strategy for a shift to a market economy, basing its approval on data and analysis provided by its secretariat. Such an approach would ease the analytical and administrative burden on both recipients and donors.

The candidates for such a role are the World Bank, the OECD, the EC Commission and the European Bank for Reconstruction and Development when it is established. The argument in favour of the World Bank is its experience of this role already, albeit among developing countries where the conditions are arguably different, its large staff and the existence of a structure which includes donors and recipients. The argument against the Bank is that it is a lender and has its own procedures which may not suit the circumstances.

The OECD Secretariat has in its favour an unrivalled capacity for structural policy analysis in developed countries. Further, the organization already has a representative structure for the 24 member countries which are responsible for the aid effort in Eastern Europe. Finally, it is not a funding organization and it may take a more balanced view of the needs of donors and recipients. The lack of direct funds may reduce its credibility with recipients.

The EC Commission is the institution which was given responsibility for coordination of OECD emergency aid to Hungary and Poland by the 1989 World Economic Summit. It is not the immediately obvious candidate for a wider role. Only 12 of the Group of 24 are members of the Community, Commission staff have no particular knowledge of Eastern Europe and some might argue that its own policies (particularly on agriculture and trade) are no guarantee of commitment to market solutions (although the 1992 initiative argues in the opposite sense). The allocation of initial responsibility may reflect no more than a US (and perhaps Japanese) wish to force

Europe to take on proportionately more of any budgetary burden. The Commission is also a donor in its own right, with its own appraisal and disbursement procedures, and as such may not be altogether objective in its approach to conditionality.

The same is likely to be true of the projected European Bank for Reconstruction and Development. It will have members from the G-24 plus the East Europeans and possibly the USSR. It will be a donor itself, but with the paradoxical role of lending public money to the private sector. This may in turn restrict its influence with East European governments. In any case it is unlikely to be a functioning institution until late 1990.

The final alternative might be to allocate the responsibility for coordination of policy by country. Thus France might coordinate action in Romania, Italy in Hungary, the US in the Soviet Union etc. Alternatively, individual countries might coordinate by policy area – the FRG for the environment etc. In either case, different approaches by individual governments could lead to inconsistent policies across countries.

The OECD Secretariat is in many ways the most attractive candidate for the task of coordination, but it is probably now too late to give it this task. That, however, puts severe pressure on the EC Commission. If it fails to set up the necessary analytical, coordination and operational capability quickly, or fails to grip its internal procedures, there is a danger that the flow of support to all of the countries of Eastern Europe will be slower and less effective than it could be.

Conclusions

On the basis of the analysis in the preceding chapters, the approaches adopted by the G-24 in Poland and Hungary have correctly identified the main immediate difficulties and are contributing towards solutions, albeit by reacting to events. Support has focused on backing up IMF programmes, debt-rescheduling in the case of Poland, providing aid for training, institution-building, technology transfer, technical assistance and the environment, as well as for more traditional areas such as export credits and project-financing.

The same broad approaches will need to be applied in Czechoslovakia and the GDR, but without the macroeconomic aspects for the Czechs and mainly, if not wholly, by the FRG in the case of the GDR. They are probably extendable to Yugoslavia, Romania and Bulgaria if and when democratic institutions begin to emerge.

The main *long-term* approach to reviving these economies, however, must lie with the private sector. Direct investment will be forthcoming only when the Western private sector is persuaded that the combination of potential profits and economic and political stability is right. A recognition of the need for a long-term approach which contributes to long-term opportunities for the private sector is what is most obviously missing from the West's response so far.

This lack largely reflects the constraints on action in the two areas which offer most long-term impact: debt relief and access to Western markets, and most particularly European markets for goods (including agriculture), services, capital and labour. The question of access also raises the question of the role of the EC and the possibility of eventual membership, as discussed in Chapter 6.

Finally, the sheer complexity of the task calls for careful coordination of G-24 support. The need for coordination will grow as the number of countries in Eastern Europe qualifying for aid grows. The Commission of the EC must consolidate its analytical and operational resources if it is to continue to carry the coordinating role.

8

LONGER-TERM PERSPECTIVES

J.M.C. Rollo

Western support must take account of the longer-term problems within Eastern Europe. The main focus of the survey so far has been the immediate help which the West can give. Where we have looked at the longer-term issues at all, the discussion has been restricted to subjects in the West's control, notably coordination of effort, debt relief and integration into the world economy. But the East European countries have set out on a very difficult path; the combination of short-term macroeconomic problems, the need for long-term systemic reform and the impact of democracy on the expectations of the people will be hard to manage. The only sure predictions are that the process will take time and that mistakes will be made – both in the reforming countries and by those trying to help from outside. The mistakes made in these countries may be punished quickly by their voters, with perhaps a consequent slowing and weakening of the reform process. It is thus essential that Western policy be adaptive. For this it needs the ability to monitor closely and the resources to respond to perceived mistakes quickly.

The correct ordering of economic reforms in Eastern Europe is not easy to determine. Chapters 3 and 4 suggested that circumstances in Eastern Europe call for a liberalization of external economic relations as well as domestic restructuring and liberalization. This recommendation stems from the need both to shift resources quickly to the internationally traded goods sector and to impose competitive pressure on domestic monopolies. But this is a high-risk strategy. All of the countries have fragile balance-of-payments and productive structures. Despite domestic deflation, the surge in imports – mainly of capital goods, but also of consumer goods – and the inevitably slower response of exports will put the balance of payments under pressure. At the same time any attempt to put CMEA trade on a hard-currency basis is likely to worsen the position as the price of raw material imports rises, and the price and volume of manufactured exports to other CMEA countries fall. The balance of payments may therefore take longer to stabilize, putting exchange rates under greater pressure than expected.

Nor will the effects be felt solely on the balance of payments. Downward pressure on the exchange rate could undermine anti-inflationary policies, with consequent need for unpopular domestic deflation. At the same time the price and quality pressures from imports, combined with the need to be cost-competitive on world markets, will increase unemployment to new and unexpectedly high levels.

The lower economic activity and higher unemployment will reduce tax revenue and increase the demand for expenditure. Tax reform, however, particularly any shift towards income and profit taxes, could reduce revenue further. Nor can privatization programmes be expected to increase revenue in the short term.

Finally, if the productive sector does respond quickly to competitive pressures, if output recovers, exports boom, inflation is reduced and unemployment is stable and falling, these countries may then confront an infrastructure constraint. Transport and communication systems, in particular, are poor, and large-scale investment may be needed on roads, railways and telecommunications. These need not all be public-sector investments, but most of them will be.

The response of the newly emerging electorates in Eastern Europe to these potential problems and dangers is the main unknown. For the time being they seem resigned to severe falls in living standards and increased unemployment, but if austerity stretches on for years rather than months, if living standards continue to decline rather than improve and if market reforms are accompanied by increasing inequalities of income, there might be a backlash. Similarly a privatization process that favoured the existing management, which is drawn from the *nomenklatura*, or that sold off national assets cheaply to foreigners, might provoke a reaction. New governments committed to slower or even no reform might then be elected. Worse still, a popular backlash, combined with Western pressure to maintain the pace of economic reform, might lead to more authoritarian and nationalistic governments in Eastern Europe.

The risk of a reform programme and democracy going wrong somewhere will increase as the number of countries involved increases. The Western countries are committed by the G-24 statement of 16 February 1990 to extend the programme for Poland and Hungary to Czechoslovakia, the GDR, Yugoslavia, Romania and Bulgaria. The Soviet Union, as noted in Chapter 5, is in the wings. And even if it does not as a whole qualify for extensive Western help, some of the republics may do so if they break away. The Baltic states of Lithuania, Latvia and Estonia, in particular, may become test-cases sooner rather than later. It is the Balkan states, however, that present the immediate challenge.

The situation in each of the Balkan countries is serious – indeed desperate is not too strong a description for the situation in Yugoslavia and Romania. But the problems and circumstances are different, which complicates the Western approach further. Yugoslavia in particular has not yet announced multi-party elections. That lack of progress on democratic institutions, in spite of its long membership of Western multilateral organizations (GATT, IMF, World Bank, OECD) and its series of IMF programmes, makes Yugoslavia difficult to fit into the framework of G-24 aid.

Elections are planned in Romania and Bulgaria in May 1990. So their democratic credentials will then be more clearly established than those of Yugoslavia. The political situation in both, however, is still unclear, as is the economic situation. Both countries are in deep crisis, but their crises are of a different sort. Bulgaria is in a classical debt crisis; Romania, by contrast, is in crisis precisely because $10 billion worth of debt has been repaid during the 1980s. Romania now has no debt, but the cut in imports required to reach this target has left it with a depleted production structure and a standard of living closer to those of a Third World country than anywhere else in Eastern Europe.

It is likely therefore that increased numbers of countries and increased diversity will complicate the nature of the Western response. At the same time each of the East European countries will be conscious of what is being done by the West elsewhere in Eastern Europe. Thus, in designing aid for and reacting to events in each country, it will be necessary for Western countries to consider the implications for neighbouring reforming economies. This is another version of the moral hazard problem discussed in Chapter 6. Poor performance should not be rewarded with softer aid conditions for fear of encouraging others to relax the effort.

In conclusion, the East European countries have enormous potential; they also face an enormous reconstruction task. The preceding chapter put emphasis on the need for a long-term Western commitment to the reforming nations of Eastern Europe as long as they maintain democratic political systems and move towards a market system. This chapter has noted the long period which this economic reform is likely to take, the exposure to external shocks, the uncertainty over the correct ordering of reform and hence the likelihood of mistakes along with the diversity of situations in these countries. These concerns all indicate the need for Western support to be flexible and coordinated if it is to be effective.

This brings us forceably back to the conclusion of Chapter 7 about the need for coordination. The IMF will be centrally involved in analysing macroeconomic problems and coordinating short-term balance-of-payments aid. The World Bank will be a major source of medium-term aid tied to policy reforms as well as of infrastructure finance. The European Investment Bank will also be involved in project finance. The European Bank for Reconstruction and Development, when it comes into being, will reportedly restrict itself to supporting private-sector initiatives. The EC Commission will have the role of coordinating G-24 bilateral programmes as well as managing its own programme of project and training aid.

To pull this diversity together needs a central analytical and coordinating organization which can act quickly and independently. The rather specialist role of each of the individual organizations, their own financial responsibilities and no doubt a certain amount of organizational rivalry make it difficult to select any one agency as the obvious choice for this coordinating body. The OECD, as noted in Chapter 7, has many of the desirable characteristics, but because of its role in leading the G-24 effort, the EC Commission seems the most probable candidate. Whichever organization is finally responsible, it must establish control of analytical and directing functions quickly, and persuade all of those involved in the process of supporting reform to concentrate their efforts through the coordinating framework. It may need the intervention of Economic Summit leaders to give sufficient weight to this issue.

Inevitably, the first responses to the accelerating changes in Eastern Europe are reactive. But if the prize of a democratic Eastern Europe, and the concomitant of improved European and hence world security, are to be grasped, then Western support must be well designed, adaptive and available rapidly.